FREE SPEECH

WHAT EVERYONE NEEDS TO KNOW®

FREE SPEECH

WHAT EVERYONE NEEDS TO KNOW®

NADINE STROSSEN

OXFORD
UNIVERSITY PRESS

OXFORD
UNIVERSITY PRESS

Oxford University Press is a department of the University of Oxford. It furthers
the University's objective of excellence in research, scholarship, and education
by publishing worldwide. Oxford is a registered trade mark of Oxford University
Press in the UK and certain other countries.

"What Everyone Needs to Know" is a registered trademark of
Oxford University Press.

Published in the United States of America by Oxford University Press
198 Madison Avenue, New York, NY 10016, United States of America.

Library of Congress Cataloging-in-Publication Data
Names: Strossen, Nadine, author.
Title: Free speech : what everyone needs to know / Nadine Strossen.
Description: New York : Oxford University Press, 2024. |
Series: What everyone needs to know; vol. 1 |
Identifiers: LCCN 2023026350 (print) | LCCN 2023026351 (ebook) |
ISBN 9780197699652 (paperback) | ISBN 9780197699645 (hardback) |
ISBN 9780197699669 (epub) | ISBN 9780197699683
Subjects: LCSH: Freedom of speech—United States. |
United States. Constitution. 1st Amendment.
Classification: LCC KF4772.S77 2023 (print) | LCC KF4772 (ebook) |
DDC 342.7308/53—dc23/eng/20230608
LC record available at https://lccn.loc.gov/2023026350
LC ebook record available at https://lccn.loc.gov/2023026351

DOI: 10.1093/wentk/9780197699645.001.0001

Paperback printed by Sheridan Books, Inc., United States of America
Hardback printed by Bridgeport National Bindery, Inc., United States of America

This book is dedicated to Salman Rushdie, whose unparalleled courage and eloquence in defending and exercising freedom of speech continue to inspire. The book's epigram is an unforgettable statement I heard Rushdie make at his first post-fatwa public appearance, at a Columbia University celebration of the First Amendment's bicentennial on December 11, 1991. I am recasting these memorable words only slightly, to match the What Everyone Needs to Know® series's question-and-answer format.

"[Isn't] freedom of speech . . . a nonstarter?" [asks] one of my Islamic extremist opponents.

No, sir, it is not. Free speech is the whole thing, the whole ball game. Free speech is life itself.

TABLE OF CONTENTS

4. Speech restrictions that the First Amendment permits

5. Speech restrictions that the First Amendment bars

ACKNOWLEDGMENTS

Deep thanks are due for the following valued contributions: for researching and drafting endnotes and a list of additional recommended readings—FIRE (the Foundation for Individual Rights and Expression) staff members Margaux Granath and Matt Harwood, and FIRE interns Nia Cain, Justin Crosby, Charlie Hatcher, Dylynn Lasky, Emma Maple, Manas Pandit, Daniel Shaw, and Vydalia Weatherly;[1] for comments on the manuscript—Ron Collins, Bob Corn-Revere, Joel Gora, Jacob Mchangama, and Brad Smith; for research assistance—Amara Banks, Yasmine Boto, Michael McCarthy, and Sean Stevens; for assistance with the endnotes and other supplementary materials on the NYLS website, Regina Chung; and for patient, creative problem-solving with computer technology, Jason Buckweitz.

For generating the questions and stimulating the answers in this book, I am indebted to the thousands of students and audience members, as well as many academic and activist colleagues, with whom I have been discussing these issues throughout my career.

For unflagging encouragement and support concerning this book, I especially thank my husband Eli M. Noam and my literary agent Carol Mann.

I am also deeply grateful to Niko Pfund, David McBride, Lari Heathcote, Wendy Walker, and everyone else at Oxford University Press and Newgen who contributed to the editorial and production process.

INTRODUCTION

Controversies about free speech have long pervaded our political and cultural spheres. Beyond the profound matters of principle that have engaged society's most brilliant philosophers throughout history, freedom of speech also entails innumerable practical public policy matters at all levels of governance worldwide, from local school boards to the United Nations.

Seemingly everyone agrees that free speech is good and censorship is bad; in all my countless debates against proponents of just about every speech restriction that has been advocated in the past 50 years, almost all of them have praised free speech and condemned censorship. But while there may be a consensus on those conclusions, there is no consensus on what we mean by either free speech or censorship, let alone on any of the more specific questions at issue. For instance, advocates of hate speech restrictions maintain in good faith that they are promoting free speech, on the rationale that those restrictions will amplify the voices of people who otherwise would be subject to hate speech and hence deterred from expressing themselves. But opponents of hate speech restrictions likewise maintain in good faith that they are promoting free speech, because such restrictions will mute much important expression, including expression by members of minority groups; for instance, powerful political leaders recently have condemned Black Lives Matter advocacy as "hate speech" (as well as "disinformation" and "terrorist" speech). Indeed, the more one wrestles with these issues, the more one appreciates their complexities, which are not fairly reducible to a speech-versus-censorship dichotomy.

Promoting constructive debates about free speech

Debates about all aspects of free speech and censorship, including the very meaning of those concepts, will no doubt continue. Indeed, especially for all of us who support free speech—however we might understand it—that inevitability is positive, exemplifying free speech in action. These debates will be most fruitful, though, if they are based on sound information about the pertinent facts and issues, including the current tenets of First Amendment law, and the actual impacts of free speech and censorship in various contexts, including in various countries and historical periods.

Both anecdotal and survey evidence indicates that there is significant hostility toward certain core First Amendment principles, but that this hostility reflects a misunderstanding of those principles. The hostility is actually aimed at a distorted, caricatured version of those principles. Correspondingly, people tend to become more supportive of free speech when they learn what the current speech-protective principles actually are, and the history that led to them.

Let me cite one key example. Critics of free speech regularly lambaste supposed "free speech absolutists," including some Supreme Court Justices, who purportedly reject any speech restrictions at all and even maintain that speech can do no harm. Yet the reality is that even—indeed, especially—the strongest free speech proponents recognize speech's great power, which necessarily can do great harm, as well as great good. Correspondingly, even the strongest free speech proponents support limits on the most dangerous speech: speech that directly, imminently causes or threatens certain specific serious harms, such as by intentionally inciting violent conduct that is likely to happen imminently. Moreover, advocates of robust free speech recognize that speech may well contribute to significant harm even if it doesn't satisfy this so-called emergency standard, but free speech advocates also recognize the dangers of vesting government with increased censorial powers.

In fairness, it must likewise be acknowledged that proponents of particular speech restrictions are also too often inaccurately characterized—in their case as "censors"—without recognizing that they are committed to free speech in general, but reach different conclusions about the comparative harms of permitting and restricting specific speech.

Once participants in free speech debates are aware of the actual speech-protective and speech-restrictive principles that the Supreme Court has enforced, and the actual positions that various advocates espouse, the debates can shift from the false binaries of free speech versus censorship to the real issues: Which speech should be restricted, and under what circumstances?

Knowledge is power

This intentionally short book necessarily is confined to the broad principles and analytical approaches that govern specific controversies, but it does not lay out how judges and other policymakers have enforced these general guidelines in all of the myriad particular situations in which they arise. As the book explains, the resolution of each case is highly fact-specific, turning on all the pertinent facts and circumstances. In many cases, different decision makers—including various Supreme Court Justices—reach different conclusions about how the governing standards apply in the specific context at stake.

On the one hand, readers might well be frustrated by the absence of straightforward, simple answers to particular free speech questions. On the other hand, though, I hope that readers will see the more complicated free speech reality as empowering. Once you are conversant with the governing general guidelines, you are as well positioned as anyone else to analyze and advocate how those guidelines should apply to any specific factual scenario. Furthermore, once you realize that there is no single, simple correct resolution of most free speech controversies, you should have the self-confidence to formulate and voice your own views about them. I hope you will exercise your free speech rights to do so.

Consistent with the mission of Oxford University Press's *What Everyone Needs To Know®* series, this book seeks to offer "a balanced and authoritative primer" on free speech. Accordingly, I write this book in my role as a free speech scholar and educator, not as a free speech advocate. Nonetheless, education about free speech tends to promote its protection in two ways. First, evidence shows that the more accurate information people have about free speech principles, history, and impact, the more supportive they are likely to become. Second, knowledge about free speech is a prerequisite for its defense. Freedom of speech is not self-enforcing, and government officials can get away with violating it unless they are held accountable for doing so. For victims of free speech violations to take corrective action, they must of course be aware of such violations; in other words, they must know what their rights are.

Notwithstanding my belief and hope that readers will become more supportive of free speech by virtue of knowing more about it, in the true spirit of free speech, I would consider my educational efforts a failure if I did not stimulate critical thinking about all the answers to all the questions in this book. My goal for every reader is the same goal I have set for all my law students: You should be able not only to answer every question, but also to question every answer.

While this book addresses "what everyone *needs* to know about free speech," it also presents "what everyone *wants* to know about free speech," because it reflects the tens of thousands of questions on point that people have been asking me, throughout my adult lifetime. Accordingly, I have written this book in the mode of listening to and dialoguing with interested members of the public, rather than lecturing to—or, worse yet, preaching at—you. I hope that, at least for most readers, this book responds to your most pressing questions.

So, let the book's questions and answers—and the additional questions and answers I hope they will provoke—begin (but never end!).

1

FREE SPEECH FUNDAMENTALS

A threshold question: What is this book's overall structure?

The book begins with some introductory questions and answers about the importance of freedom of speech, which highlight the universal and timeless support for—and opposition to—it. Accordingly, the book explains how this fundamental concept transcends the First Amendment to the U.S. Constitution—indeed, how it transcends any law or legal system, by encompassing cultural elements as well. That said, the First Amendment constitutes one of the longest-lasting legal sources of free speech protection,[1] which has had an enduring, worldwide impact. Both its language, and the Supreme Court's many cases interpreting it, have influenced the free speech protections and limits that subsequently have been incorporated into the law of many other countries, as well as international and regional human rights treaties. For these reasons, this book focuses on the First Amendment's language and the Supreme Court's precedents enforcing it.

First Amendment free expression law is notoriously complicated, consisting of hundreds of Supreme Court decisions spanning more than a century, some of which are in tension—if not squarely inconsistent—with each other. The Supreme Court lays out First Amendment law on a case-by-case basis, and the Court can't control what lawsuits are initiated, let alone which lower court rulings will be presented to it for review.

Therefore, there are important First Amendment issues that it has not considered, or has not reconsidered for a long time, despite significant intervening legal and factual developments. Moreover, the Court has declined to address certain issues even when they are presented in cases on its docket. For these reasons, any generalization about the Court's rulings is subject to qualifications and exceptions. Given this book's intentionally short length, it highlights the broad patterns and themes in First Amendment law, and the underlying rationales they reflect, while omitting the details and caveats that would be included in a legal brief or law review article.

Before discussing the major precepts of First Amendment law individually, the book provides a broader overview, by answering the following two questions: "What are the five most important facts that everyone needs to know about freedom of speech?" and "What are the 12 most important, most challenging arguments against the strong free speech protection in current First Amendment law, and what are the strongest counterarguments?"

The answers to the first question preview central aspects of First Amendment law that subsequent answers explore in more detail. The answers to the second question highlight the major themes that have emerged through the Supreme Court's evolving First Amendment case law. These themes broadly unify an enormously variegated body of decisions, and undergird the modern Court's general trend toward more robust speech protection across many specific free speech law issues, which began to gain momentum in the 1960s.

What's the relationship between "freedom of speech" and the "First Amendment"?

Many people use the term terms "freedom of speech" and "First Amendment" interchangeably, but these two terms refer to distinct concepts.[2] First Amendment free speech rights constitute a subset of the more wide-ranging concept of freedom of speech to which individuals worldwide long have aspired.

The First Amendment provides important protection for "the freedom of speech" vis-à-vis U.S. officials, but even within the United States, the general concept of speech freedom extends beyond that protection. For example, students and faculty members at most private colleges and universities can expect their academic institutions to protect their basic free speech rights, such as the right to criticize campus policies, but these rights are secured by other sources of law, not the First Amendment (because the First Amendment does not impose obligations on private sector entities). Additionally, the general concept of free speech has been embraced by people all over the world, throughout history, wholly apart from any legal protections. Indeed, the U.S. government is premised on the view that free speech—along with other "unalienable rights"—is a "natural" human right, with which we are "endowed" by virtue of our humanity, and that the purpose of our laws and government is "to secure" that preexisting right (the quoted phrases are in the Declaration of Independence and the Constitution).

No matter how speech-protective our laws might be, freedom of speech still will not be a vital reality unless we reinforce free speech law with a free speech culture, in which individuals actually exercise and support free speech. The British writer George Orwell underscored this essential real-world dimension of free speech: "If large numbers of people believe in freedom of speech, there will be freedom of speech even if the law forbids it. But if public opinion is sluggish, inconvenient minorities will be prosecuted, even if laws exist to protect them."

Why does "everyone need to know" anything about free speech?

Why do we "need to know" anything more than that the First Amendment protects freedom of speech?

To "know" the abstract generalization that the First Amendment protects freedom of speech is no substitute for appreciating the infinite array of specific expression—including some that is deeply important to each reader personally—that depends on the strong speech-protective principles now embodied in First Amendment law, but that was subject to punishment and suppression throughout most of American history. Too many of us who have the privilege of living in the contemporary United States (and other countries with strong free speech protection) take for granted the robust but hard-won freedom of speech for which countless people have struggled and sacrificed throughout history and around the world, even putting their very lives on the line.

In the United States, although freedom of speech has been explicitly guaranteed since the First Amendment's ratification in 1791, it wasn't consistently protected until the second half of the 20th century. Before then, the First Amendment was regularly ignored and violated with impunity by government officials ranging from police officers to presidents, who predictably stifled speech with which they disagreed, including speech advocating progressive causes: abolition, women's suffrage, reproductive freedom, labor rights, antiwar movements, socialism, civil rights, and LGBTQ+ rights.

Not until 1925 did the Supreme Court recognize that the First Amendment imposes any limits at all on speech violations by state and local officials, which were rampant. And not until 1965 did the Supreme Court first strike down a federal law under the First Amendment, although Congress had a long history of passing such laws, dating all the way back to the infamous 1798 Alien and Sedition Acts, which criminalized criticism of government officials, a preeminently important type of speech in our democratic republic. As recently as the 1960s, civil rights demonstrators were regularly punished for their efforts to peacefully protest racial apartheid, which is why Martin Luther King wrote his historic "Letter from Birmingham Jail"; far from government protecting Dr. King's free speech rights and those of his allies in the civil rights movement, it punished them for daring to (try to) exercise these rights.

To this day, advocates of human rights and democracy in many other countries continue to face imprisonment or worse simply for seeking to convey their ideas. They necessarily recognize that freedom of speech is the essential engine for promoting their causes (as well as any other cause). Cherian George, who was born in Singapore and is a professor at Hong Kong Baptist University, contrasted this view among Asian human rights activists with the views of their American counterparts, after he spent a semester as a visiting professor at the University of Pennsylvania in 2018:

> In the activist circles that I inhabit in Asia, the left (including feminists and those fighting for minority rights) is solidly aligned with free speech advocates, because they know from experience that whenever speech is restricted, they suffer disproportionately. Perhaps the American left feel they can afford to be blasé, even reckless, about free speech, because they know that when they really need it, the First Amendment will be there for them. It's a risk that progressives in most of the rest of the world can't afford to take.

Why do we all need to know about free speech, regardless of our political beliefs?

There are many ongoing threats to free speech even in the United States, including threats to speech that is consistent with progressive values—for instance, state laws that seek to stifle peaceful protesters, or that bar the teaching of certain subjects or perspectives concerning race and gender in K-12 public schools, or even in higher educational institutions. Therefore, progressives in the United States—along with the "progressives in most of the rest of the world" to whom Professor George referred in the above quote—also can't afford to risk losing the safety net that First Amendment law has provided for their expression. The same is true for all of us, no matter who we are or what we believe.

Given the wonderful diversity of our pluralistic society, no matter what your identities or ideologies might be, some of your views will be seen by some other members of our society as wrong and even evil and dangerous. You will not be able to depend on majority support for all of your ideas at any particular level of government. Maybe your ideas on a particular issue might be popular in your local community, but they might well be unpopular in a larger community, or vice versa. For example, the favored policy views of progressive college students might be popular in their campus community, but deeply unpopular even in the city where the campus is located, let alone at the state or national level. In some contexts, concerning some cherished views that we seek to express, all of us will inevitably depend on the First Amendment's shield against "the tyranny of the majority."

It is often quipped that most people support "freedom of speech for me, but not for thee." The clear lesson of free speech law, and the history that gave rise to it, is that there can be no freedom of speech for me unless there is also freedom of speech for thee.

Will knowing about free speech have any positive tangible impacts on your life?

Knowledge about general free speech principles is essential for understanding and participating in the many current debates about particular free speech issues. More generally, knowledge about your own free speech rights should encourage you to vigorously exercise those rights in order to gain all the benefits that free speech promises—ranging from your own self-expression of who you are and what you feel, to conveying your ideas about political issues so that you can affect how those issues are resolved.

Knowledge is power, and even people who are disempowered in other ways—for instance, not enjoying the right to vote—have been able to express themselves, and also to successfully influence issues of concern to them, because they were aware of their free speech rights. Many students who are too young to vote have prevailed in lawsuits against school officials who sought to prevent the students from engaging in certain kinds of expression, because the students were aware of their rights (and, accordingly, sought legal assistance from supportive lawyers or organizations).

One recent illustration is the Supreme Court's 2021 decision protecting the free speech rights of high school student Brandi Levy. The Court held that Brandi's school had violated those rights when it disciplined her for Snapchat messages she had posted to her friends on her cellphone, expressing her anger toward certain school officials for actions that she considered unfair. In one fell swoop, she was able to enjoy the diverse benefits of multiple types of expression: the self-expression of "blowing off steam" through her strongly worded messages, including repeated uses of "the F-bomb"; communicating with her friends; and critiquing school officials' actions. Furthermore, Brandi's knowledge and advocacy of her own free speech rights has had a positive impact on students' free expression rights nationwide, given the precedential impact of the Court's decision in her case, limiting schools' power to punish students' speech that takes place away from school settings, including via social media.

People who exercise their free speech rights often attest to the liberating, empowering experience—whether they speak out individually or participate in a mass demonstration. At the very least, there is the satisfaction that flows from being true to oneself by openly conveying one's identity and convictions. And there is also a likelihood that one is thereby helping to ensure that "the moral arc of the universe . . . bends toward justice," in Martin Luther King's poetic phrase.

What are reasons for protecting free speech?

Around the world and across time, free speech proponents have advanced multiple reasons for protecting it. The most important include:

- Enabling individual self-expression, ranging from conveying identities—through means such as clothing, hairstyles, and tattoos, as well as words—to venting emotions, to signaling support for certain causes;
- Facilitating democratic self-government through the exchange of information and ideas among government officials, candidates, and their constituents;
- Promoting the search for truth through research, analysis, and debating ideas and evidence;
- Advancing the peaceful resolution of conflicts at all levels, through discussion and negotiation, rather than violence and war; and
- Furthering other human rights, as well as all other causes, through advocacy, lobbying, and litigating in support of such causes.

Testimonials to the essential role that free speech played in advancing their causes have been voiced by leaders of every equal rights movement throughout U.S. history, from the 19th-century abolitionist movement to the 21st-century movement for LGBTQ+ rights. Let me quote just two examples. The first is the eloquent abolitionist champion Frederick Douglass, who had been born into slavery in 1818 and escaped in 1838. In 1860, he declared: "Slavery cannot abide free speech. Five years of its exercise would banish the auction block and break every chain in the South." In 2019, law professor Dale Carpenter, a lifelong champion of LGBTQ+ rights, wrote: "It's no stretch to say that . . . [t]he First Amendment created gay America . . . [I]t . . . protected gay cultural and political institutions from state regulation. . . . No other [constitutional right] helped us more."

Beyond free speech's formidable instrumental power, free speech also enables each of us to explore, develop, and express our individual human identities and capacities. In the Supreme Court's words: "The right to think is the beginning of freedom, and speech . . . is the beginning of thought." In the same vein, recall 17th-century philosopher Rene Descartes's famous phrase: "I think, therefore I am." If we combine these two potent ideas, the logical sequence is: "I speak; therefore I think; therefore I am." The flipside of this enduring insight was chillingly conveyed in George Orwell's dystopian novel *1984*. In the totalitarian state of Oceania, the "Newspeak" language reduced people's vocabulary, precisely in order to reduce their ability to think. By eliminating certain words, the goal was to eliminate the "subversive" concepts these words conveyed.

Is free speech a universal right, recognized in all countries?

The Universal Declaration of Human Rights (UDHR), which the United Nations General Assembly adopted without dissent in 1948, proclaims: "Everyone has the right to freedom of opinion and expression; this right includes freedom to hold opinions without interference and to seek, receive and impart information and ideas through any media and regardless of frontiers." Likewise, the regional human rights treaties that have been adopted in Africa, the Americas, and Europe all contain similar language ensuring freedom of speech (the Asian countries have not adopted such a regional treaty). Finally, most countries have national constitutions or other sources of law that embody free speech guarantees. Even if some of those provisions constitute mere "lip service" because government officials do not actually honor them in practice, they demonstrate that free speech is universally recognized as an ideal.

The universal nature of freedom of speech, as reflected by its inclusion in the UDHR, means that it is considered a right to which all human beings are inherently entitled, solely by virtue of their humanity; the right is not created or bestowed by the UDHR (or other treaties, constitutions, or laws), but rather, the UDHR recognizes this innate right and pledges UN efforts to secure it. This parallels the natural rights concept incorporated in the U.S. Declaration of Independence and Constitution.

Although free speech is universally recognized as a right in theory, it is too often honored in the breach by actual government policies, including in advanced democracies such as the United States. Throughout most of U.S. history, government officials blatantly violated freedom of speech, with no meaningful judicial check until the mid-20th century. Even to this day, government officials across the United States and across the ideological spectrum regularly violate free speech rights, as attested by the regular stream of court rulings that strike down these actions under the First Amendment.

No rights guarantees are self-executing; instead, constant activism is required to ensure that government officials actually honor them. For any government official to respect free speech rights, and for any individual to take whatever action is needed to secure governmental respect—such as lobbying or litigating—the first prerequisite is knowledge about the right. In short, "everyone needs to know about free speech" so that free speech can become a universal right not only in theory, but also in reality.

Is free speech a right that has been protected—or sought to be protected—throughout history?

Yes! Historians have traced arguments favoring freedom of speech, and government policies that have recognized aspects of such freedom, in every historical period, dating back to ancient times.

A recent, comprehensive account is *Free Speech: A Global History from Socrates to Social Media*, a 2022 book by Jacob Mchangama, the founder and director of the Danish think tank

Justitia. The book explores the constant human striving for free speech and resistance to censorial powers throughout history, and also around the world. An opening passage provides the following summary:

> [T]he roots of free speech are ancient, deep, and sprawling. The Athenian statesman Pericles extolled the democratic value of open debate and tolerance of social dissent in 431 BCE. In the ninth century CE, the irreverent freethinker Ibn al-Rawandi used the fertile intellectual climate of the Abbasid Caliphate to question prophecy and holy books. In 1582 the Dutchman Dirck Coornhert insisted that it was "tyrannical to . . . forbid good books in order to squelch the truth." The first legal protection of press freedom was instituted in Sweden in 1766 and Denmark became the first state in the world to abolish any and all censorship in 1770.

Mchangama's book explores the ancient origins of the philosophical justifications for free speech in Athens and Rome. It documents the continuing free speech aspirations even during what it terms "the not-so-Dark Ages," discussing both "inquiry and inquisition" in the medieval Islamic realm, as well as medieval Europe. Of the many free speech champions it quotes, from many ages and regions, I will cite just one example: Mahatma Gandhi, who hailed freedom of speech and its cognate freedom of assembly as the "two lungs that are absolutely necessary for a man to breathe the oxygen of liberty."

The eternal, universal nature of human beings' free speech aspirations is also underscored by another salient fact: Throughout history, in countries with every kind of political system, courageous individuals have advocated for free speech, even at great personal risk, including imprisonment and execution. From Socrates choosing death by poison, to protesters against repressive regimes today, to religious "heretics" throughout the ages, countless human beings with widely varying beliefs have preferred death to a life devoid of free speech and the integrally interrelated freedom of conscience. As the acclaimed writer and free speech champion Salman Rushdie said in the 1991 statement that is this book's epigram: "Free speech is life itself." Given the mortal danger he has heroically faced since the Ayatollah Khomeini's 1989 *fatwa* (religious edict) instructing Muslims to kill him, and the increasing bounty on his head, for Rushdie free speech literally is a life-and-death matter. More recently, speaking from his prison cell upon receiving the Nobel Peace Prize in 2010, Chinese human rights activist Liu Xiaobo eloquently described this precious freedom, for which he had sacrificed his physical liberty: "Free expression is the foundation of human rights, the source of humanity, and the mother of truth."

What are the five most important facts that everyone needs to know about freedom of speech?

Some evidence indicates that knowledge about freedom of speech tends to increase support for it. Below I list five key facts about speech freedom that should serve this function. The listing constitutes a preview; later questions and answers throughout this book explore these points in more detail.

1. The First Amendment permits government to outlaw the speech that is the most dangerous, consistent with the "emergency" principle: speech that, considered in its overall context, directly, imminently causes or threatens specific serious harm.
2. The First Amendment outlaws the censorship that is the most dangerous: restrictions based solely on disfavor of the speaker's ideas, or on generalized, speculative fear that the speech might indirectly contribute to some future harm.

3. Although speech that doesn't satisfy the emergency principle ("non-emergency speech") may well potentially cause harm, it is dangerous to grant government the added latitude to punish speech with a less direct, imminent connection to potential harm; predictably, government (which is accountable to majoritarian and other powerful interest groups) disproportionately exercises any such discretion to suppress minority voices and views.

4. While non-emergency speech restrictions seek to reduce the potential harm of the targeted speech, such restrictions do not necessarily lead to a material reduction in either the targeted speech or its potential harm, and in fact they may well do the opposite—for example, by increasing the attention and sympathy that the speech receives.

5. Many experts have concluded that counterspeech—any expression that counters the potential harmful impact of non-emergency speech, including information and persuasion—can be a more effective "harm reduction" strategy than censorship, parallel to expert conclusions regarding drug prohibition. In both contexts, the potentially harmful ideas/substances can never be eliminated; therefore, the more promising approach is to increase people's resistance to them.

2

THE MOST IMPORTANT ARGUMENTS FOR AND AGAINST FREE SPEECH

What are the 12 most important, most challenging arguments against the strong free speech protection in current First Amendment law, and what are the strongest counterarguments?

Having been studying, educating, advocating, discussing, and debating free speech issues intensely throughout my professional career, I have repeatedly considered countless questions about and arguments against free speech. The same relatively small group of questions/arguments are the most common, because they are the most important and the most challenging.

1. Isn't First Amendment law too rigidly absolute?

A widespread misconception about U.S. law's speech-protective norms is that they absolutely protect all speech. In fact, modern Supreme Court decisions—starting in the second half of the 20th century—have generally interpreted the First Amendment as permitting the government to outlaw the speech that is the most dangerous, while also outlawing the censorship that is the most dangerous. This approach reflects two fundamental general principles, which have been supported by Justices all across the ideological spectrum: (1) the viewpoint (or content)[1] neutrality requirement; and (2) the emergency test.

What speech restrictions does the First Amendment outlaw?

Later answers will outline specific kinds of speech restrictions that the First Amendment bars, but the present answer will focus on the preeminently important general principle of viewpoint (or content) neutrality, which the Supreme Court has hailed as the "bedrock principle underlying the First Amendment." In its landmark 1972 decision that first expressly set out this principle, *Police Department of Chicago v. Mosley*, the Court declared: "[A]bove all else, the First Amendment means that government has no power to restrict expression because of its message, its ideas, its subject matter, or its content." No matter how deeply and widely loathed the message might be, this does not justify censoring it. Rather, we must use alternative means to counter the message, including education and persuasion.

The Supreme Court has explained that any viewpoint-based speech regulations would subvert not only individual liberty, but also our democratic self-government, due to the inherent danger that officials would enforce such regulations to "suppress unpopular ideas or information or manipulate public debate."

Viewpoint-based speech restrictions also violate equality norms, because official discrimination against certain ideas entails discrimination against certain speakers. As far back as 1951, the Court acknowledged these intertwined forms of discrimination when it struck down a city's refusal to grant a Jehovah's Witnesses group a permit to use a park for Bible talks, even though it had granted such permits to other religious and political groups. The Court observed that "the permit was denied because of the city's dislike for or disagreement with the Witnesses." And in *Mosley* itself, the Court invoked the Constitution's Equal Protection Clause, as well as the Free Speech Clause, in striking down a Chicago ordinance that outlawed picketing on certain topics, which had been wielded to punish a Black postal worker's peaceful picketing against racial discrimination.

Notably, the *Mosley* opinion was written by Thurgood Marshall, the Court's first Black Justice, who had headed the NAACP (National Association for the Advancement of Colored People) Legal Defense and Educational Fund. The *Mosley* case illustrates a significant pattern in the Court's speech-protective rulings, which will be evident throughout this book: Many of these decisions, regarding multiple specific free speech issues, protect speech by minority speakers and/or advocating equal rights causes.

In sum, "above all else," the First Amendment bars viewpoint-discriminatory speech regulations because they endanger liberty, equality, and democracy alike.

What speech restrictions does the First Amendment permit?

In contrast, the government may regulate speech for reasons other than its disfavored message, so that "there is no realistic possibility that official suppression of ideas is afoot." On this rationale, government may punish expression whose message directly and immediately inflicts an independent harm (i.e., beyond the disfavored nature of its ideas), including bribery, copyright infringement, defamation, fraud, perjury, and quid pro quo sexual harassment. For example, fraud causes financial injury, and perjury undermines the justice system.

In addition, consistent with the emergency principle, the government may restrict speech when, under all the facts and circumstances, the speech directly, imminently *threatens* certain specific, serious harm (even if it does not directly and immediately cause such harm). In all of these situations, the justification for restricting the speech goes beyond its content, to consider its context. (This book uses the term "emergency," which the Supreme Court has not specifically defined as a constitutional law term of art, to encompass all of the just-described speech—speech that either immediately causes harm or threatens to do so imminently.)

The Supreme Court has laid out context-specific criteria for several categories of speech that government may restrict consistent with the emergency test. One example is a "true threat": when the speaker directs the expression to one person or a small group, and intends to instill a "reasonable" or objective fear of harm on the part of the targeted person(s). Other examples of context-based categories of speech that satisfy the emergency principle include intentional incitement of imminent violent or lawless conduct that is likely to happen imminently, and targeted harassment or bullying that infringes upon the targeted individuals' privacy or freedom of movement. Additionally, expression that is part of a conspiracy to commit illegal or violent acts may be criminally punished, as well as subject to a civil action for damages by victims of such acts.

What are recent examples of hate speech that may be punished, consistent with the First Amendment?

Speech with a controversial message, such as hate speech or extremist speech, may be punished when it satisfies the contextual standards that comply with the emergency principle. For instance, in August 2017, when hundreds of Unite the Right demonstrators in Charlottesville, Virginia, menacingly crowded in upon a small group of counterdemonstrators on the University of Virginia campus while brandishing lighted tiki torches, the demonstrators' expression constituted punishable threats; the marchers intentionally instilled in counterdemonstrators a reasonable fear that they would be subject to harm. Moreover, nine people who had been injured during the demonstrations successfully sued two dozen white nationalists and organizations involved in spearheading the threats and violence; in 2021, a jury held the defendants culpable of conspiracy and imposed $25 million in damages upon them.

Although the viewpoint-neutrality principle bars government from punishing hate speech solely due to its hateful—and hated—message, hate speech often constitutes evidence that facilitates convictions under "hate crimes" statutes. These statutes, which exist in almost every state and also at the federal level, increase the penalties for crimes when the perpetrator intentionally selects a crime victim for discriminatory reasons; that discriminatory intent is generally demonstrated through the perpetrator's hate speech that is closely connected to the crime. For example, on the basis of such hate speech, the murderers of Ahmaud Arbery—who killed him while he was jogging through their neighborhood in Glynn County, Georgia—were found guilty on federal hate crimes charges in 2022.

2. Even speech that doesn't satisfy the emergency standard ("non-emergency speech") could well be harmful, so why doesn't the First Amendment permit non-emergency speech restrictions?

This especially important question seeks—and challenges—the rationales for the First Amendment concept of unconstitutional censorship. Because "censorship" has no specific legal meaning, throughout this answer I instead use the term "non-emergency speech restrictions" to highlight the specific distinction between permissible and impermissible speech restrictions under the First Amendment. (In the remainder of the book, I sometimes use the shorthand "censorship" to designate the non-emergency speech restrictions that violate the First Amendment.)

The answer to this important, challenging general question also applies to multiple specific questions throughout this book, including why the First Amendment bars non-emergency restrictions on speech with various kinds of controversial content, such as hate speech, disinformation/misinformation, and speech that causes emotional distress. Therefore, the overall answer to this key question is the longest and most detailed answer in this book. That said, both this question and its answer are logically divisible into several subquestions and answers. Before laying these out, though, I will first summarize the overall answer to the overall question.

Speech that doesn't satisfy the emergency standard ("non-emergency speech") by definition doesn't directly, imminently cause or threaten specific serious harm. For that very reason, such speech isn't necessarily harmful in any particular instance. To be sure, non-emergency speech is potentially harmful, but that harmful potential doesn't justify non-emergency speech restrictions. Moreover, even if non-emergency speech were in fact harmful in any particular situation, it would not necessarily have a net harmful impact in the aggregate—that is, considering all the situations in which it had a positive impact, as well as those in which it had a negative impact.

Even if we assumed (completely hypothetically) that non-emergency speech *did* have a net harmful impact in the aggregate, non-emergency speech restrictions still would not necessarily be warranted. Rather, such restrictions would only be warranted if all of the following questions were also answered affirmatively:

- Can these restrictions describe the targeted harmful speech in sufficiently clear, precise language to avoid problems of undue vagueness and substantial overbreadth, which endanger much speech that is not harmful?
- Do these restrictions materially reduce the harmful impact of the targeted speech?
- Do the restrictions' benefits, in terms of reducing the targeted speech's harmful impact, outweigh their unintended costs, such as suppressing non-targeted, non-harmful speech; increasing attention to/sympathy for the targeted speech; and disproportionately silencing marginalized voices and views?

- Are there no alternative measures, which are less speech-restrictive than the non-emergency speech restrictions, that would be as effective as these restrictions, or more so?

The logical analysis that the foregoing questions outline makes just plain common sense. While we might well tolerate restrictions on our fundamental free speech rights in order to promote some important benefit, such as decreased discrimination or violence, why should we tolerate such restrictions if they did not in fact materially promote such a benefit, or if the same benefit could be promoted through an alternative measure, which did not limit our free speech rights? Given its logical force, it is not surprising that this analysis is reflected in not only First Amendment law, but also the major United Nations treaty governing free speech, as well as the free speech law in many other countries. Here is how this analysis is formulated in the terminology of First Amendment case law: Any content-based speech restriction (i.e., a restriction that targets particular topics or ideas) is subject to judicial "strict scrutiny," requiring the government to demonstrate to the reviewing court that the restriction is "necessary"—in other words, the "least restrictive" means—for materially promoting a countervailing goal of "compelling importance."

The strict scrutiny test, which courts use to "scrutinize" or review restrictions on various constitutional rights—including freedom of speech—is essentially another way of formulating the emergency standard for reviewing speech restrictions in particular. Both rubrics demand a close connection between the speech and the feared harm, such that suppressing the speech is required to prevent the harm. The emergency test is framed in terms of the harm that the speech will necessarily cause if it is not restricted, whereas the strict scrutiny test is framed in terms of the harm that the speech restriction is necessary to prevent. To underscore this overlap between the two formulations, I will at times refer to them in tandem, as the "emergency/strict scrutiny" tests.

Even though we reasonably fear that non-emergency speech might indirectly contribute to future harm, we have even more reason to fear government power to restrict speech on that ground. Justice Louis Brandeis eloquently set out this view, and the corresponding emergency principle, in an often-quoted 1927 opinion, which the modern Supreme Court unanimously endorsed in a 1969 case: "Fear of serious injury cannot alone justify suppression of free speech. . . . Men feared witches and burnt women. . . . Those who won our independence by revolution were not cowards. . . . They did not exalt order at the cost of liberty. . . . Only an emergency can justify repression."

Now that I have set out the logical subquestions that are embedded in this difficult, complex overarching question— asking why the First Amendment bars non-emergency speech restrictions—I will address each subquestion in turn. The subquestions and answers pertain to all non-emergency restrictions on speech with any controversial content. To illustrate various points, I will refer specifically to non-emergency restrictions on hate speech, because many people advocate these restrictions in particular.

Does the harmful potential of non-emergency speech justify restricting it?

By definition, non-emergency speech does not directly and imminently cause or threaten harm; in short, it is not necessarily harmful. Of course, non-emergency speech is potentially harmful. However, as a purported justification for non-emergency speech restrictions, the claim that the speech at issue is potentially harmful proves both too much and too little. *All* speech may potentially cause a wide range of harm. Given the infinite array of circumstances in which speech is conveyed and received, and the limitless complexities of each individual's psyche and experience, any message might well have a harmful impact on at least some audience members. Supreme Court Justice Oliver Wendell Holmes well captured this reality when he noted that "every idea is an incitement," therefore rejecting the government's argument that it should be permitted to censor speech with a "tendency" to "incite" harmful conduct. Even if we confined non-emergency restrictions to expression that induced particular individuals to engage in violence, a sweeping array of expression would be endangered. There are myriad documented cases of individuals who credibly claim that they were "incited" to commit heinous crimes, including mass murders, based on their (mis)readings of everything from Dostoevsky's classic novel *Crime and Punishment*, to the Bible, to the Qu'ran.

I am writing this answer just a few days after the brutal knife attack on celebrated author Salman Rushdie (in August 2022), causing multiple severe injuries. The evidence to date indicates that the assailant was induced to commit this crime by the 1989 *fatwa* issued by Iran's then-Supreme Leader, Ayatollah Khomeini, based on his view that Rushdie's 1988 novel, *The Satanic Verses*, blasphemed the prophet Muhammad. Does this mean that the horrific attack on Rushdie (as well as prior attacks on—and murders of—others associated with *The Satanic Verses*, who were also subject to the *fatwa*) was ultimately instigated by *The Satanic Verses* itself? And/or by the Qu'ran?[2]

Just as all speech is potentially harmful, so too, no speech is predictably harmful, for precisely the same reason: Whatever impact speech has on a particular audience member depends on its intermediating processing by that individual's mind. To assume a simplistic cause-and-effect relationship even between a single, explicit statement and the recipient's reaction is to deny human autonomy and moral agency. Even if a superior military officer commands troops to shoot civilians, history shows that some troops will not follow the order. Many people who hear vicious racist speech are spurred by it not to adopt racist attitudes, much less to engage in racist conduct; to the contrary, they are galvanized to engage in antiracist activism. And some people who are targeted by disparaging slurs do not therefore feel humiliated or intimidated; instead, they look down upon or even pity the would-be disparager. As lifelong gay rights champion Jonathan Rauch wrote: "If someone calls me a 'fucking faggot,' I interpret her as telling me that she needs counseling, not that I am a fucking faggot."

Even if non-emergency speech weren't harmful in any specific instance, would it necessarily have a net harmful impact in the aggregate?

For reasons the preceding answer set out, it would be extremely difficult to quantify the myriad positive and negative impacts even of a single instance of non-emergency speech (for example, a single racist epithet) let alone an entire category of such speech (for example, racist speech or, even more broadly, hate speech). That very difficulty, though, points to a clear negative answer to this question; precisely because it is so hard to quantify the net impact of any non-emergency speech in the aggregate, it follows that this impact cannot be shown to be necessarily harmful.

I will illustrate the negative answer to this question with an odious recent hate speech incident, which some readers will vividly recall: the expression of the Unite the Right demonstrators in Charlottesville, Virginia, in 2017. Substantial elements of their expression were appropriately punishable, consistent with the emergency principle, in light of the overall context in which it was uttered—that is, as targeted threats or conspiratorial plans. But if one focuses on the non-emergency expression in which the demonstrators also engaged—such as the racist slogans they chanted, considered alone—is it clear that the expression's net impact was negative? Did that expression, on balance, recruit more white supremacist followers, or did it instead spur more antiracist government initiatives and grassroots activism?

The latter conclusion was supported by none other than Susan Bro, the mother of Heather Heyer, the counterdemonstrator who was murdered when a Unite the Right supporter ruthlessly drove his car into a crowd of counterdemonstrators. (In 2019, he was sentenced to life imprisonment plus 419 years for these crimes, and in 2021, an appellate court confirmed his conviction.) In a 2019 interview, Bro strongly supported the Unite the Right demonstrators' free speech rights specifically because she believed that the airing of their racist views should have a net positive impact on the antiracism cause for which her daughter's life had been sacrificed:

> [W]e walk into the room blindly if we don't take the time to know what the other side is thinking. . . . [H]ate groups . . . want a violent reaction or they want no one to oppose them at all. [N]either approach is effective. . . . [T]he effective approach is to show up in even larger numbers, without violence, to assertively say, "We see you, we don't like you [or] what you're saying. . . ." And we saw this in the second Unite the Right Rally in Washington when they showed up in very small numbers and . . . were met with counter protesters . . . in . . . very large numbers, saying "go home, go away."

If non-emergency speech did have a net harmful aggregate impact, would non-emergency speech restrictions be warranted?

Even if we assumed hypothetically (contrary to the preceding answers) that non-emergency speech would inevitably have a net negative impact, it still would not follow that government should restrict that speech. Logically, one could justify any such speech restriction only by analyzing additional questions about its costs and benefits, and the comparable costs and benefits of non-censorial measures. These questions are set forth and answered below.

Can non-emergency speech restrictions be written
in sufficiently clear, precise language to avoid problems
of undue vagueness and substantial overbreadth?

By definition, non-emergency speech restrictions extend to
speech that lacks a tight, direct causal connection to harm.
Non-emergency restrictions are based solely on the speech's
disfavored content, or on its more speculative, indirect connection to potential harm. In either case, the government's enforcement latitude enables it to engage in viewpoint discrimination,
singling out particular expression due to its disfavored message. This problem is exacerbated by the irreducibly subjective
concepts at the heart of all the controversial types of speech
that many politicians and others regularly advocate subjecting
to non-emergency restrictions—such as hate speech, disinfor-
mation/misinformation, and extremist/terrorist speech. Is
Black Lives Matter advocacy hate speech, and/or disinforma-
tion/misinformation, and/or terrorist/extremist speech, as influential right-leaning politicians have claimed? Is information
about the lab leak theory for the origins of the COVID pandemic hate speech (against Chinese people) and/or disinfor-
mation/misinformation, as influential left-leaning politicians
have claimed?

Due to their inherent problems of undue vagueness
and substantial overbreadth, any non-emergency speech
restrictions would have two major adverse consequences.
First, such restrictions would deter individuals from engaging
in much speech that they reasonably fear could be punished
under these nebulous and expansive concepts. Because many
of us seek to avoid even being accused of engaging in such
condemned speech, the chilling effect would inevitably silence
much valuable speech that even the restrictions' proponents
would not want to repress, including speech about matters of
public concern, which are especially important in our representative democracy. Second, officials would exercise wide-
ranging discretion, which means that the restrictions would be

enforced arbitrarily at best, discriminatorily at worst—hence reinforcing their chilling impact.

The foregoing problems with any non-emergency speech restrictions are illustrated by many countries' experiences with such restrictions on hate speech. These restrictions have been enforced to suppress much important expression about pressing public policy issues, even by politicians; ironically, they also have been enforced against counterspeech that is deliberately designed to refute hateful ideas. Recent developments in Germany are all too typical. In 2018, Germany implemented strict limits on internet hate speech as part of its new "NetzDG"[3] law, which deputized online companies to enforce Germany's preexisting nonemergency hate speech restrictions. NetzDG's first casualties included tweets by the co-leader of the far-right Alternative for Germany (AfD) party and her deputy, as well as a series of tweets from the satirical magazine *Titanic*, which parodied the deleted AfD comments. Jörg Rupp, a social worker and political activist, also had his Twitter account banned, after he invoked the language of right-wing groups to underscore their "cruelty" toward asylum-seekers. His conclusion: "It's dangerous . . . to be ironic." Likewise, one of Germany's best-known street artists, whose work often challenges the far right, had five posts deleted within the first 2 weeks after NetzDG went into effect.

Although the targeted AfD tweets used incendiary language about Muslims and immigrants, they concerned important controversies about immigration and criminal justice policies. Furthermore, no matter how abhorrent one might consider the AfD rhetoric and positions, they have significant support among the German public, thus constituting essential elements of public debate. Therefore, by suppressing both AfD speech and multiple instances of counterspeech, the NetzDG law swiftly muted both sides of critically important public policy debates.

Would such restrictions materially reduce the speech's harmful impact?

Both logical analysis and empirical evidence show that non-emergency speech restrictions are ineffective at best, counterproductive at worst. Due to their invariably vague, broad language, they are inevitably both under-inclusive and over-inclusive; they do not suppress much of the targeted harmful speech, while they do suppress substantial speech that is not targeted because it is not harmful.

Even the strictest censorship laws have never succeeded in completely stifling targeted speech. Perhaps a non-emergency hate speech restriction will induce some people who otherwise would have engaged in hateful expression to cease doing so, for fear of punishment; or perhaps they will at least cease doing so in public during any period of incarceration to which they might be sentenced.[4] Nevertheless, just as even the most severe criminal laws and penalties have hardly terminated illegal behavior—from possessing controlled substances to mass murder—it is predictable that the targeted speech will persist despite censorship laws. Even in authoritarian countries, even the most controversial speech manages to survive, propounding views that the authorities consider subversive and blasphemous. This is a testament to the universal human desire for freedom of thought and speech.

The endurance of controversial speech, notwithstanding efforts to censor it, is also a testament to the fluidity of language, and the subtle ways in which communications influence human thought and action. Despite the censorship of myriad particular words, ideas will survive, given the limitless ways in which they can be conveyed. In a September 19, 2022, article in the *Forward* entitled, "When Trump Supporters Gave Him the Finger, Was it Really a Nazi Salute?," Mira Fox chronicled not only the evolution of the gesture of pointing toward the ceiling to reference a hate group or a conspiracy theory, but also the constant development of innumerable other such oblique references:

New [hateful gestures] are invented almost constantly within the bowels of the internet as part of the churn of memes and nested references that comprise internet culture. Sometimes, even people in the know can miss the references; by the time a symbol is recognizable to more casual, less obsessive followers, it will be near the end of its life.

Plus, hate symbols are designed to look innocuous . . . and to be hard to track—that's how they escape notice from algorithmic filters and teams screening social media for hate speech.

Hate speech, as listed in the Anti-Defamation League's database, includes such basic options as "100%," which white supremacists use to reference the idea of a completely white society. . . . Other numerals, including 1, 2, 12, 13, and 14, can also be hate symbols. "Coors," a major brand of cheap, light beer—[whose current ownership] does not endorse white supremacy—can also stand for "Comrades of our racial struggle."

Even beyond the constant proliferation of particular synonyms and memes to convey certain problematic ideas, there is a further reason why censorship cannot suppress such ideas. That is because the ideas are also conveyed indirectly, through the aggregated impact of multifarious oblique references. Communications scholar Cherian George well explained this phenomenon, citing two types of controversial speech that are subject to many actual and proposed restrictions—disinformation and hate speech:

The most powerful "fake news" deceptions are not usually made up of neatly self-contained messages. For example, the well-documented misperception among most Americans that crime [had] been rising [during periods when it was in fact decreasing] cannot be attributed solely to election candidates' "pants-on-fire" lies, but is also due to factual but selective reporting by news media as well as fictional depictions of violence in entertainment media. Similarly, hate campaigns comprise disaggregated collections of historical narratives, . . . stereotypes about the Other, and curated streams of news and opinion that reinforce favored ideologies. Viewed singly, most of these messages may not cross any regulatory threshold; it is in the audience's heads that they combine to harmful effect.

Would such restrictions have unintended adverse consequences?

As noted above, just as laws in general don't completely deter the proscribed conduct, it is likewise true that non-emergency restrictions on controversial expression likewise will not completely deter all such expression. For anyone whose controversial expression is not wholly deterred, non-emergency restrictions afford three options, all of which undermine the restrictions' goals. First, some such expression will be driven underground, thus reducing opportunities for discovering and dissuading those who purvey or heed it, and also undermining law enforcement officials' efforts to monitor it in order to detect, deter, and disrupt any planned illegal or violent actions. Second, some such expression will be camouflaged in more subtle rhetoric to evade punishment, thereby making the speech more appealing to a broader audience. Third and finally, some such expression will remain unchanged, or perhaps even ramped up, as the speakers seek the publicity and sympathy that regularly result from suppression efforts; due to the well-documented "forbidden fruits" or "boomerang" phenomenon, censored material tends to garner increased interest and support.

Beyond the multiple counterproductive impacts of non-emergency speech restrictions already mentioned—suppressing non-targeted, non-harmful speech, including even counterspeech; making it more difficult to refute the speech and to disrupt planned illegal conduct; and increasing attention to and support for the targeted ideas and speakers—there is yet another important counterproductive impact, which is predicted by logic and confirmed by longstanding international experience. The government leeway inherent in non-emergency speech restrictions constitutes a license to punish views and speakers that the government disfavors. Before the Supreme Court's adoption of the speech-protective emergency principle in the second half of the 20th century, government was permitted to punish speech with a harmful potential or "bad tendency." Unsurprisingly, government consistently exercised this broad discretion to suppress speech by members of marginalized minority groups and advocates of causes that contemporaries viewed as dangerous, from abolition of slavery to LGBTQ+ rights.

Are there less speech-restrictive alternatives, which would be at least as effective as the non-emergency speech restrictions?

While evidence casts doubt on the efficacy of non-emergency speech restrictions, it also supports the efficacy of non-censorial alternative measures. Since the restrictions focus on expression, they constitute only superficial "quick fixes" that don't really fix the actual problems: the underlying discriminatory attitudes and resulting actions. Correspondingly, more effective measures do address discriminatory attitudes and actions. These include antidiscrimination laws; laws against "hate crimes" or "bias crimes," which target crimes whose victims are singled out for discriminatory reasons; and "counterspeech," which constitutes any speech that counters hateful ideas, including by proactively promoting positive countervailing values.

Human rights advocates in countries that enforce hate speech laws have endorsed these alternative non-censorial approaches on the ground that they are more effective than censorship. For instance, in 2017 the European Centre for Press and Media Freedom issued a statement opposing increased German restrictions on hate speech, explaining: "Combating illegal incitement to violence, hatred, . . . and discrimination is indeed . . . crucial. . . . But . . . censoring speech has never [been] shown to be effective: it is rather by more speech . . . that our societies will be helped."

What lessons can we learn from criminal law reform?

Laws that criminalize or otherwise punish certain controversial (but non-emergency) speech have much in common with laws criminalizing other actions that are harmful to individuals and society. All such laws seek to deter the harmful behavior and to reduce its harmful impacts. Recently, there have been many reform efforts in our criminal law system, with support from officials all across the political spectrum. The expert consensus is that our system has been too harshly punitive, overly relying on criminal law responses to individual and societal problems that are more effectively countered through alternative strategies. Experts have concurred that disproportionately harsh approaches may well increase perpetrators' antisocial attitudes and behaviors, rather than the opposite. They have instead advocated "harm reduction" and "restorative justice." These alternative strategies have been supported and implemented in response to even the most serious, violent crimes, including murder. It seems only logical that such strategies should also be pursued in response to problematic speech.

Censoring speech is a "prohibition" strategy, seeking to dry up the supply and consumption of the dangerous item— in this case, controversial speech—by punishing those who supply and consume it. As with other famously failed prohibition strategies, such as the War on Drugs, experts concur that punitive supply-side efforts are futile. Rather, they maintain, the most constructive response is to reduce people's demand for the targeted item, and also to reduce its harmful impact on them. In the case of drugs, that means sufficiently educating people to the drugs' harmful impact, so that they will be deterred from ingesting the drugs; but if people nonetheless become drug abusers, they should receive effective treatment. In the case of hate speech and other potentially harmful expression, the demand-side harm reduction strategy is persuading people not to listen to the speech, or if they do listen, to reject its message and resist any potential harmful impact it could have. For example, mental health experts say that all of us can be trained to be resilient in the face of speech that is potentially upsetting, insulting, and traumatizing, such as hate speech. As another example, even leaders of overtly discriminatory organizations have been "redeemed" (their own term) through extended communications with people who patiently engage with them, gradually leading them to question and ultimately reject their former views. Organizations such as Life After Hate enlist hundreds of such "formers" (again, their own term) to reach out to others who are still active in hateful organizations, or who are sympathetically considering the organizations' ideas, to "redeem" them as well. Likewise, to cite one final example, communications experts agree that all of us can learn information literacy and critical media skills, so that we can recognize disinformation/misinformation and hence disregard and discount it.

3. Doesn't First Amendment law wrongly privilege freedom of speech above equality rights?

Far from privileging freedom of speech above equality rights, U.S. law treats both as "fundamental" rights, which are equally entitled to the strongest constitutional protection. Accordingly, the First Amendment permits speech restrictions that are necessary to promote equality. To illustrate the relationship between free speech and equality rights, this answer will focus on hate speech.

Hate speech may be restricted under several contextually defined categories of speech that comply with the emergency principle. In such circumstances, the speech restriction has been deemed necessary to promote equality. Conversely, when courts have struck down particular hate speech restrictions as unconstitutional, the evidence has not supported this conclusion. To the contrary, human rights advocates worldwide have complained that many hate speech restrictions, far from promoting equality goals, may well undermine them—by vesting enforcing officials with undue discretion, which they foreseeably use disproportionately to silence speech by and on behalf of the very minority groups who were the laws' intended beneficiaries.

When may government restrict speech in order to promote equality?

On the one hand, no right—including fundamental rights such as free speech and equality—is absolute. On the other hand, every fundamental right—including both free speech and equality—is strongly protected against any government measure that substantially burdens or restricts it. The government bears the burden of vindicating any such measure under the "strict scrutiny" test: Government must demonstrate that the restriction materially promotes a countervailing goal of compelling importance and is necessary to do so; if the goal could be furthered through an alternative measure, which is less restrictive of the right, the government must instead pursue that alternative. It is usually easy for the government to show that a challenged rights-restricting measure aims to promote a sufficiently important goal, but the government often has a hard time showing that the measure even materially advances that goal, let alone is necessary/the least restrictive alternative for doing so.

Enforcing fundamental rights is, of course, a goal of compelling importance. Therefore, if a restriction on free speech were necessary/the least restrictive alternative to promote racial (or other forms of) equality, that restriction would pass constitutional muster. That is why the First Amendment permits the government to restrict expression that constitutes racially discriminatory harassment: when the expression targets an individual or small group of individuals based on their race and "harries" or annoys them, interfering with their privacy and liberty. Likewise, restrictions on racist expression that constitutes "hostile environment" harassment in an educational or employment setting are also constitutional: racist expression that is so objectively offensive, severe, and pervasive that it denies equal educational or employment opportunities on the basis of race. In both situations, the specific speech restrictions are necessary/the least restrictive alternative for promoting racial equality.

Consistent with the emergency principle, hate speech restrictions can also satisfy strict scrutiny when they are necessary/the least restrictive alternative to prevent specific harm that the speech directly, imminently causes or threatens. A vivid example is certain expression by the Unite the Right marchers in Charlottesville in 2017, which constituted punishable "true threats"; the speakers meant to instill reasonable fear on the part of directly targeted counter-demonstrators that they would be subject to violence.

Why shouldn't government have even more power to restrict speech with the aim of advancing equality?

If government could show that an additional proposed restriction on hate speech, beyond the examples cited above, not only was designed to promote equality, but also was necessary/the least restrictive alternative for doing so, that restriction would be constitutional. Experience has shown, however, that whenever enforcing authorities have discretion to impose speech restrictions that don't satisfy the strict scrutiny/ emergency tests, the authorities predictably tend to exercise that discretion in ways that entrench already powerful speakers and groups, and that excessively silence those who have been traditionally marginalized. For this reason, human rights advocates in many countries and in international organizations have opposed such expanded hate speech laws. For example, in 2016, some members of the United Nations Human Rights Committee stated: "In many countries, [hate speech] rules . . . are abused by the powerful to limit non-traditional, dissenting, critical, or minority voices, or discussion about challenging social issues. Hate speech . . . laws ironically are often employed to suppress the very minorities they purportedly are designed to protect."

In sum, to conclude that hate speech restrictions are unconstitutional when they fall short of the strict scrutiny/emergency tests is not to elevate free speech rights above equality rights. Rather, these restrictions are unconstitutional precisely because they do not sufficiently advance equality rights, but instead may well undermine them.

Other restrictions on other kinds of speech—beyond hate speech—that are also designed to promote equality would have to be analyzed separately, consistent with the First Amendment's fact-specific analysis. For example, several Supreme Court decisions unanimously rejected First Amendment challenges to laws requiring formerly all-male organizations to admit women, notwithstanding the organizations' argument that this would undermine their "freedom of expressive association." Although the Supreme Court has recognized this implicit First Amendment freedom, under the circumstances of these cases, it deemed that freedom to be outweighed by the countervailing equality concerns.

4. Doesn't freedom of speech rest on the flawed assumption that words are harmless?

No! Speech is protected precisely because of its powerful potential to affect hearts, minds, and actions; that power may contribute to either good or harm. In a 2011 case the Supreme Court acknowledged evidence that the speech at issue—hateful insults aimed at particular individuals and groups, including LGBTQ+ people, military personnel, and Catholics—caused emotional distress to the plaintiff (whose deceased son was the target of some of this disparaging expression), with associated adverse physiological impacts. Nonetheless, the Court concluded that the speech could not be punished, in light of other considerations: It took place on public streets, which constitute "traditional public forums" that (to quote a 1939 decision) "have immemorially been held in trust for . . . purposes of . . . communicating thoughts between citizens, and discussing public questions"; and it addressed matters of public concern, which have always been considered of utmost importance in our representative democracy. The Court stated: "Speech is powerful. It can stir people to action, move them to tears of both joy and sorrow, and—as it did here—inflict great pain. . . . [W]e cannot react to that pain by punishing the speaker. As a Nation we have chosen a different course—to protect even hurtful speech on public issues to ensure that we do not stifle public debate."

Even when non-emergency speech is harmful, that factor alone would not validate non-emergency speech restrictions. Rather, as a matter of logic, several additional factors must also be taken into account, including whether the restrictions would actually be effective in mitigating the speech's harmful potential, rather than counterproductive, and whether less speech-restrictive alternative measures would be at least as effective. In a nutshell, the First Amendment is premised not on the flawed assumption that words are harmless, but rather on the evidence- and analysis-based premise that even if speech is harmful, non-emergency speech restrictions might well be more harmful.

5. Doesn't freedom of speech rest on the false premise that the marketplace of ideas will lead to truth?

This argument has two major flaws. First, the truth-seeking rationale for freedom of speech never has depended on the clearly meritless view that good ideas will necessarily dominate, while bad ideas will necessarily evaporate. Rather, the truth-seeking rationale has depended on the demonstrably valid view that we can better approach this ideal result through a vigorous exchange of ideas among members of the public rather than any top-down control. Second, even assuming hypothetically that the truth-seeking rationale were unpersuasive, robust free speech protection would still be justified on the basis of one or more of the additional, independently sufficient rationales that underpin it.

As a truth-seeking mechanism, how does the marketplace of ideas compare to alternative approaches?

The truth-seeking rationale rightly constitutes one important justification—albeit only one among several—for contemporary speech-protective standards. Although this rationale dates back to much earlier free speech philosophers, it was first encapsulated in the memorable marketplace metaphor in a landmark 1919 dissent by U.S. Supreme Court Justice Holmes, whose reasoning was later endorsed by the modern Court. (Holmes did not use the precise phrase "the marketplace of ideas," but he did advert to that concept.) Consistent with Holmes's skeptical philosophical outlook, he hypothesized that the free exchange of ideas might be a better alternative than "persecution for the expression of opinions," explaining: "[W]hen men have realized that time has upset many fighting faiths, they *may* come to *believe* . . . that the ultimate good desired is *better* reached by free trade in ideas— that the *best* test of truth is the power of the thought to get itself accepted in the competition of the market" [emphasis added].

As the italicized words indicate, Holmes's argument was far from an outright prediction that free speech would inevitably lead to truth. Rather, he explained, "the *theory* of our Constitution" is that free speech is better suited for truth-seeking than censorship, but he acknowledged that this approach "is an *experiment*, as all life is an experiment," since it is necessarily "*based upon imperfect knowledge*" [emphasis added]. Nonetheless, Holmes concluded:

> While that experiment is part of our system, . . . we should be eternally vigilant against attempts to check the expression of opinions that we loathe and believe to be fraught with death, unless they so imminently threaten immediate interference with the lawful and pressing purposes of the law that an immediate check is required to save the country.

In short, a rigorous search for truth demands that all ideas must be subject to debate and discussion through robust free speech—including that very concept itself.

Since Holmes wrote those memorable words, more than a century ago, evidence accumulated through our ongoing First Amendment "experiment" continues to reaffirm that free speech is a less imperfect vehicle for pursuing truth than is the censorial alternative. For instance, in 2021, scientific evidence came to light supporting the previously discredited theory that COVID had originated from a leak in a Wuhan, China, laboratory. Government officials and experts had condemned this theory as "fake news" and even "hate speech" (against Chinese people) since the pandemic's outbreak in early 2020, and it had been suppressed in major traditional and social media outlets. Yet in the spring of 2021, the theory was rehabilitated as at least deserving serious consideration. Despite this theory's exclusion from key segments of the marketplace of ideas, that overall marketplace was still functioning. Had that not been the case, we would have been denied critically important on-going assessments, with their potentially enormous impact on public health and national security.

In 1984, Professor Melville Nimmer well captured the core skeptical, relativistic notion underlying the truth-seeking rationale for free speech. Referring to Holmes's above-quoted language, he asked: "If acceptance of an idea in the competition of the market"—i.e., among the public at large—"is not the 'best test' of its truth, what is the alternative?" Logically, as he concluded, the answer could "only be acceptance of an idea by some individuals or group narrower than that of the public at large"—that is, some subset of the public. Are "We the People," who wield sovereign power in our democratic republic, willing to entrust any individual or group with the incalculable power of determining which ideas are fit for our consideration and discussion? Are we willing to entrust that power to any government official or body? The legal historian Michael Kent Curtis, writing about early-19th-century abolitionists' preference for free speech versus censorship as a strategy, ascribed that preference to this same least-bad analysis:

> Given the human tendency to reject unorthodox ideas and to screen out those that do not confirm pre-existing notions, the vision of truth easily conquering error is too optimistic. But without tight controls on censorship of ideas, truth may be deprived even of a fighting chance.

Are there other rationales for free speech, beyond the marketplace of ideas?

In addition to the truth-seeking rationale for strongly protecting free speech, there are multiple other rationales, each of which provides an independent justification for such protection. These include its essential roles in promoting democratic self-governance, individual autonomy, tolerance, the peaceful resolution of conflicts, and all other human rights.

6. Isn't freedom of speech the tool of the powerful, not the powerless?

People who have access to resources that facilitate communication—including money, education, and technology—can more vigorously exercise their freedom of speech to communicate more effectively with a larger audience. That fact, however, does not logically support the conclusion that freedom of speech should be curtailed. Rather, it supports the conclusion that our society must continue to vigorously promote everyone's full and equal access to the means for effective communication.

In 1960, journalist A. J. Liebling famously quipped that "[f]reedom of the press is guaranteed only to those who own one." Advocates of both free speech and equal rights have been working to change that impoverished free speech reality, including by leading the fight for a free and open internet, which can potentially make everyone the functional equivalent of a printing press owner. The Supreme Court celebrated this liberating, equalizing potential of online expression in its landmark 1997 decision that upheld robust free speech rights in the then-new online context: "Any person with a phone line can become a town crier with a voice that resonates farther than it could from any soapbox." The internet and mobile phones have empowered grassroots groups to mobilize for multiple causes—including Black Lives Matter and #MeToo— that could not have gained such traction through the vastly more expensive, exclusionary communications tools of earlier eras. Likewise, many young, relatively unknown political candidates—including women and members of racial, ethnic, religious, and other minority groups—have harnessed the relatively cheap, accessible social media platforms to campaign successfully.

It is sad but true that not only freedom of speech, but also other rights, are too often more fully enjoyed by those with more resources. The solution to this problem is hardly to reduce the scope of the rights, but rather, to increase the ability of more people to actually exercise them. Consider, for instance, the fundamental right to life itself. In the United States, people charged with capital crimes are far more likely to be sentenced to death, and actually executed, if they are indigent and hence dependent on overburdened and under-resourced public defenders. The answer to this problem is not to decrease constitutional protections that constrain capital punishment, but instead to increase the resources that permit non-wealthy people to benefit from them. Likewise, in the free speech context, we must ensure the educational, techno-logical, and other resources that will enable everyone to actu-ally enjoy free speech as a real-life experience, not merely an abstract legal right.

There is another fatal flaw in the argument that freedom of speech further entrenches the privilege and power of those who already have both: It is precisely those who lack polit-ical or economic power who are the most dependent on robust speech freedom. Throughout U.S. history (and in other coun-tries), equal rights and social justice movements have gained momentum through forceful exercise of free speech rights to advocate and demonstrate, litigate and lobby. Conversely, cen-sorship consistently has been wielded to stymie these causes. These patterns are no coincidence. Elected officials are predict-ably responsive to majorities or powerful interest groups, so the Constitution enshrines rights such as freedom of speech precisely to protect unpopular individuals and marginalized minorities from "the tyranny of the majority," as illustrated by many of the Supreme Court decisions that this book summarizes. To this day, state and local governments around the United States have been disproportionately enforcing ex-isting laws, and enacting new ones, to stifle protesters for pro-gressive causes that challenge the status quo, including racial justice, environmental equity, and police reform. In short, it is the disempowered, not the powerful, who have the most to gain from strong free speech protection, and the most to lose from its weakening.

7. Isn't some speech tantamount to violence, and therefore subject to punishment, along with other forms of violence?

Physical violence directly and inevitably causes some physical harm, as well as associated psychic harm. Speech does potentially cause or contribute to psychic and physical harm. Unlike physical violence, though, speech can influence listeners only through their intermediating perceptions and reactions, and only as one of countless other factors that also have potential influence. For this reason, hurling words at someone is materially different from hurling the proverbial "sticks and stones." Sticks and stones directly cause harm, through their own force, but words at most can potentially contribute to harm; whether particular words actually do cause harm depends on how individual listeners perceive and respond to them, which in turn is influenced by innumerable other factors. In sum, while it is certainly not true, to quote the old nursery rhyme, that "words will *never* hurt me," it is equally untrue that they will *always* do so.

When there is a sufficiently tight and direct causal nexus between speech and specific serious harm, including violence, such speech may be punished, consistent with the emergency principle. For instance, government may punish a speaker who intentionally incites imminent violence that is also likely to happen imminently. As another example, under the "fighting words" doctrine, government may punish a direct, face-to-face personal insult that is intended and likely to provoke an immediate violent reaction. As yet another example, when a speaker addresses an individual or small group of individuals and intentionally instills in the audience members a reasonable fear that they will be subject to violence, that is a punishable "true threat" (even when the speaker doesn't intend to actually carry out the threatened violent act).

In contrast, when government has been allowed to punish speech because of a more speculative, attenuated connection between it and some potential future violence—as happened in the United States in the past, and as still occurs in other countries—government foreseeably exercises this discretionary power to punish disempowered speakers and dissenting perspectives. In the United States, major targets included socialists and communists, as well as civil rights activists, even when they pursued only peaceful, nonviolent strategies for achieving social change.

For instance, in the 1963 *Edwards v. South Carolina* decision, the Supreme Court overturned "breach of the peace" convictions, which had been imposed by a South Carolina trial court and affirmed by the South Carolina Supreme Court, on a group of high school and college students who had peacefully marched on the state capitol grounds, "carrying placards bearing such messages as 'I'm proud to be a Negro' and 'Down with Segregation,' and singing the Star Spangled Banner and other patriotic and religious songs." The U.S. Supreme Court observed that the students "were convicted upon evidence which showed no more than that the opinions which they were peaceably expressing were sufficiently opposed to the views of the majority of the community to attract a crowd and necessitate police protection."

Today's student equal rights advocates often claim that "speech is violence" when the speech is inconsistent with their worldviews. They would probably be surprised to learn that this very same argument was made in an effort to silence their ideological forebears: student equal rights advocates in an earlier generation. To cite another example, a 1965 Supreme Court decision, *Cox v. Louisiana*, overturned a Black minister's criminal conviction for leading a group of Louisiana college students in a peaceful pro–civil rights demonstration, based in part on a police officer's testimony that "the students were 'violent' because they . . . do things that disrupts [sic] our way of living down here." In the same vein, the trial judge said that the minister's breach-of-the-peace conviction—and his 21-month prison sentence, plus a $5,500 fine (equivalent to about $52,000 in 2023)—was justified because it is "inherently dangerous . . . to bring 1,500 . . . colored people [to] the predominantly white business district in . . . Baton Rouge and . . . sing songs . . . carrying lines such as 'black and white together.' . . . That has to be an inherent breach of the peace."

Even today, powerful critics of Black Lives Matter and other social justice activists seek to suppress and punish their expression on the ground that it allegedly constitutes or causes violence. Yet the modern Court has protected the use of violent rhetoric that falls short of the emergency test by advocates of wide-ranging causes, including civil rights and antiwar movements. A noteworthy example is a 1969 case arising from the Vietnam-era military draft, in which the Court held that the First Amendment protected the following statement by an 18-year-old Black man, Robert Watts, despite its violent language. Referring to then-President Lyndon Baines Johnson, Watts said: "If they ever make me carry a rifle the first man I want to get in my sights is L.B.J. They are not going to make me kill my black brothers." Watts was convicted of threatening the president. However, characterizing Watts's statement as "political hyperbole," the Supreme Court reversed his conviction, explaining that "[t]he language used in the political arena . . . is often vituperative, abusive and inexact."

I will cite one more example of pro–civil rights speech that benefited from the modern Court's protection of violent rhetoric that falls short of the emergency standard. In the 1982 *Claiborne Hardware v. NAACP* case, the Court held that NAACP officials had a First Amendment right to threaten violent reprisals against violators of an NAACP-organized boycott of racially discriminatory white merchants (which dated back to 1966). NAACP field organizer Charles Evers had warned boycott violators: "If we catch any of you going in any of them racist stores, we're gonna break your damn neck." Although several Black people who patronized white merchants were subsequently subject to violent attacks, the Court held that Evers's words did not satisfy the demanding test for punishable incitement of violent conduct, because the violence did not occur "imminently." The Court observed that we must tolerate such violent language because "strong and effective extemporaneous rhetoric cannot be nicely channeled in purely dulcet phrases. An advocate must be free to stimulate his audience with . . . emotional appeals."

Blurring the critical distinction between speech and violence not only leads to unjustified speech suppression; it also leads to unjustified violence. When constitutionally protected speech is assailed as "violent," not surprisingly, violent reprisals are also rationalized as simply "tit for tat." Alarmingly, in a 2022 survey by FIRE (the Foundation for Individual Rights and Expression) and College Pulse, more than one in four college students (27%) said that it is acceptable to use violence to some degree (either "always," "sometimes," or "rarely") to shut down a controversial speaker.

The savage August 2022 knifing attack on author Salman Rushdie should highlight the dramatic distinction between wielding words—even disparaging words that could chill other speech—and wielding weapons with the aim of permanently, completely silencing a human being. Even beyond the tragic temporary silencing of Rushdie himself, this kind of brutal attack also has a boundless censorial impact on the countless others who are frightened into self-censorship—no doubt a major motive for the attack.

8. Hasn't freedom of speech become mostly a conservative talking point?

It is true that too many conservatives are eager to support free speech when conservative speakers or views are the targets of censorship—but less eager to support free speech in other circumstances. That said, the same is also true for too many liberals and progressives. To quote again the familiar quip, most people believe in "free speech for me (or people who agree with me), but not for thee."

In contrast with the general public, modern Supreme Court Justices across the ideological spectrum have regularly supported freedom "even for the thought that [they] hate," which Justice Holmes extolled as the constitutional principle "that more imperatively calls for attachment than any other." Although the Justices have been deeply divided on many constitutional law issues, they have generally been strongly united in supporting free speech even for the most controversial expression, which large segments of the public favor suppressing. Liberal Justices have supported free speech even for white supremacists' racist and anti-Semitic rants, and conservative Justices have supported free speech even for a communist who expressed his contempt for the United States by burning the American flag. Likewise, along with the Justices, human rights lawyers and organizations have consistently supported freedom even for expression that conveys ideas antithetical to their own equal rights principles. Probably the most (in)famous example is the American Civil Liberties Union (ACLU)'s 1977–78 defense of free speech for neo-Nazis demonstrating in Skokie, Illinois, the home of many Jews, including many Holocaust survivors.

Why do so many Justices and human rights lawyers strongly support robust freedom of speech, including the core viewpoint-neutrality principle, in contrast to so many members of the general public? This disparity may well be explained by a key factor that distinguishes members of the legal profession from the general public: Members of the legal profession are familiar with First Amendment principles, as well as the history that gave rise to them. Therefore, lawyers and judges have witnessed that, whatever speakers and ideas might be the immediate beneficiaries of speech-protective

principles in a particular case, those same principles also re-
dound to the benefit of very different speakers and ideas in
other cases. Conversely, lawyers and judges have seen that
granting government more authority to restrict speech, under
less speech-protective principles, endangers all speakers and
ideas—but none more so than marginalized speakers and dissident ideas. As an ACLU brief in the Skokie case pointed out,
the very same speech-protective principles that permitted the
neo-Nazis' provocative march in a community where their
ideas were viewed as hateful and dangerous had also permitted "Martin Luther King, Jr.'s confrontational march into"
another Illinois community—Cicero. In 1966, *Time* magazine
described Cicero as "a Selma[, Alabama,] without the Southern
drawl." Accordingly, many of Cicero's officials and other
residents viewed the ideas of the pro–civil rights marchers as
hateful and dangerous.

Before the Supreme Court adopted its speech-protective
approach, censorship was used to stifle speech with a wide
array of messages, including the advocacy of many liberal and
progressive causes. Conversely, the Court's modern speech-
protective cases have facilitated those very same causes. Many
of the leading modern First Amendment precedents arose from
the mid-20th-century civil rights movement. The Supreme
Court repeatedly struck down speech-suppressive measures
that civil rights foes deployed in an effort both to silence civil
rights advocates themselves and to prevent the national media
from conveying their message to the larger, critically important national audience. As the great civil rights champion
and longtime Congressman John Lewis observed: "Without
freedom of speech, the civil rights movement would have been
a bird without wings."

To this day, equal rights and other social justice activists
have been subject to censorial measures that seek to stifle
their advocacy. For instance, governments have been enacting
and enforcing multiple measures that curb rights of peaceful
protesters, and police have deployed speech-suppressive

tactics, including unjustified force and arrests. Fortunately, the ACLU and other free speech defenders have been able to successfully challenge these repressive measures, but that's thanks to the robust free speech principles that also protect the rights of people with diametrically different views.

9. Doesn't Germany's experience, with the rise of Hitler and Nazism, show that we should censor hateful and extremist speech?

Given the horrors of the Holocaust, even diehard free speech stalwarts would support censorship that could have averted that atrocity. That is certainly the case for me, as the daughter of a German-born Holocaust survivor, who narrowly escaped being murdered at Buchenwald. That also is true for the prominent international human rights champion Aryeh Neier, who managed to flee from Nazi Germany with his immediate family when he was a child, while the Nazis slaughtered his extended family. Neier was the ACLU's executive director in 1977–78, when the ACLU successfully defended the First Amendment rights of neo-Nazis to demonstrate in Skokie, Illinois, with its large Jewish population, including many Holocaust survivors. Because Neier is a justly renowned free speech proponent, many readers will be surprised to learn of his statement that he would have supported censoring the Nazis if that would have forestalled their ascension to power:

> I am unwilling to put anything, even love of free speech, ahead of detestation of the Nazis. . . . I could not bring myself to advocate freedom of speech in Skokie if I did not believe that the chances are best for preventing a repetition of the Holocaust in a society where every incursion on freedom is resisted. Freedom has its risks. Suppression of freedom, I believe, is a sure prescription for disaster.

Proponents of non-emergency restrictions on hate speech regularly invoke the assumption that the enforcement of such restrictions might have prevented the spread of Nazi ideology in Germany. The historical record, though, belies this assumption. Throughout the Nazis' rise, there were laws on the books criminalizing hateful, discriminatory speech, which were similar to contemporary hate speech laws in Germany and elsewhere. This fact was cited by Alan Borovoy, general counsel of the Canadian Civil Liberties Association, when he set out his/the CCLA's opposition to Canada's current hate speech legislation:

> Remarkably, pre-Hitler Germany had laws very much like the Canadian anti-hate law. Moreover, those laws were enforced with some vigour. During the fifteen years before Hitler came to power, there were more than two hundred prosecutions based on anti-Semitic speech. And, in the opinion of the leading Jewish organization [in Germany] of that era, no more than 10% of the cases were mishandled by the authorities.

The German hate speech laws were enforced even against leading Nazis, some of whom served substantial prison terms. Rather than suppressing the Nazis' anti-Semitic ideology, these prosecutions helped the Nazis gain attention and support. For instance, Danish journalist Flemming Rose reports that between 1923 and 1933, the virulently anti-Semitic newspaper *Der Stürmer*, published by Julius Streicher, "was either confiscated or [its] editors [were] taken to court on . . . thirty-six occasions." Yet, "[t]he more charges Streicher faced, the greater became the admiration of his supporters. The courts became an important platform for Streicher's campaign against the Jews."

The major problem with Germany's response to rising Nazism was not that the Nazis enjoyed too much free speech, but that the Nazis literally got away with murder. In effect, they stole free speech from everyone else, including anti-Nazis,

Jews, and other minorities. As Neier commented in his classic book about the Skokie case: "The lesson of Germany in the 1920s is that a free society cannot be . . . maintained if it will not act . . . forcefully to punish political violence. It is as if no effort had been made in the United States to punish the murderers of Medgar Evers, Martin Luther King, Jr. . . . and . . . other victims" of violence during the civil rights movement.

10. Aren't free speech defenders wrong when they claim that the best answer to harmful speech is "counterspeech"?

"Counterspeech" is a shorthand term for any speech that seeks to counter or reduce the potential adverse impacts of controversial speech, including hate speech. A major form of counterspeech is education or information dispelling the ideas and attitudes that the problematic speech reflects. Examples of speech designed to reduce the potential sting of hateful or discriminatory expression include proactive education that instills values of tolerance and support for equal human rights for all; responsive information and analysis to refute advocacy of discriminatory policies; and supportive communications to individuals who have been disparaged by hate speech. Many individuals and organizations have developed a dazzling array of creative, innovative counterspeech strategies to curb the harmful impact of an equally broad array of controversial speech, drawing upon every mode of expression—including art, humor, and satire—and employing multiple communications technologies, including algorithmically generated responses to online questions and comments.

Doesn't counterspeech unfairly burden members of minority groups who are targeted by hate speech?

Concerning hate speech in particular, those who advocate censorship regularly raise several objections to counterspeech, which all miss the mark. First, contrary to common misconceptions, counterspeech should not be the responsibility of individuals or groups who are targeted by hate speech. Nor should counterspeech be limited to defensive responses to hate speech. Rather, all of us who are committed to resisting hatred and discrimination should seize every opportunity proactively to advocate equality, dignity, diversity, and inclusion.

To be sure, some individuals who have been subject to hate speech have recounted their positive, empowering experiences when they have chosen to respond to the speech in various ways—ranging from disputing the discriminatory ideas, to organizing counterdemonstrations in the face of hatemongers' rallies, to walking away from a hateful speaker. Likewise, multiple minority group leaders have encouraged individuals who have been targeted by hate speech to raise their own voices in opposition, as a way to reinforce their personal sense of dignity and empowerment.

I will cite one example that is especially compelling because it dates back to the early 1990s, when—according to the trailblazing advocates of campus hate speech codes at that time—there was almost no acknowledgment of hate speech, let alone counterspeech against it, by campus leaders or anyone else. This example stems from a racist speech incident at Arizona State University in 1991. According to ASU Law Professor Charles Calleros, who was closely involved in the situation, a "racially degrading poster" had been displayed on the outer door of a room in a campus dormitory. Calleros recounted that the "four black women students" who noticed the poster engaged in constructive counterspeech with the occupant of that room, as well as others on campus, and this episode became the springboard for university-wide antiracism initiatives.

In addition to the four Black women who initially saw the poster, these initiatives were spearheaded by another student, Rossie Turman, in his capacity as chair of ASU's African American Coalition. Turman commented: "When you get a chance to swing at racism, and you do, you feel more confident

about doing it the next time. It was a personal feeling of empowerment, that I don't have to take that kind of stupidity."
Had the response instead been punitive, a contemporaneous *Progressive Magazine* editorial opined, that would have served to "increase the dependency of . . . victims of hate and oppression. Instead of empowering them, [a punitive response] enfeebles them." Although disparaged individuals and groups may well choose to engage in counterspeech and consider that a positive experience, as in the ASU situation, it is worth repeating that they bear no responsibility to pursue this option, let alone the primary responsibility.

All supporters of full and equal human rights should promote vigorous educational and other efforts that will equalize actual opportunities to engage in speech, specifically including counterspeech. For example, psychologists maintain that all of us can learn how to react to speech that seeks to disparage us not with negative feelings about ourselves, which result in stifling our voices, but rather with self-confidence and resilience, which emboldens our voices. It is especially essential to ensure that educational, technological, and psychological resources are deployed to extend free speech opportunities to those whose voices traditionally have been muted. University of Pennsylvania Professor Sigal Ben-Porath coined the apt term "inclusive freedom" to connote the ideal of meaningful freedom of speech for all—a freedom that everyone can equally enjoy, rather than a mere theoretical promise that only a privileged few can actually exercise.

Isn't counterspeech "only words"?

Critics of counterspeech often belittle its potential positive impact by noting that counterspeech constitutes "only words." Yet the same point could be made about hate speech itself (as well as other controversial expression). Censorship proponents cannot have it both ways. Either words are ineffectual, in which case hate speech (or other controversial speech) doesn't cause enough harm to warrant censoring it; or words are powerful, in which case they can do good, as well as harm.

In fact, the pioneering law professors who initially advocated non-emergency restrictions on hate speech in the United States starting in the 1980s—Richard Delgado, Charles Lawrence, and Mari Matsuda—consistently bemoaned the lack of counterspeech at that time, contending that counterspeech would significantly reduce hate speech's harmful impact. Likewise, human rights champions have cited the absence of counterspeech as having significantly hampered their causes in earlier times. For instance, during the civil rights movement, Martin Luther King, Jr. said: "In the end, we will remember not the words of our enemies, but the silence of our friends." And the influential international human rights leader Aryeh Neier credited anti-Nazi speech with having spared some European Jews during the Holocaust, while he correspondingly blamed the absence of such speech for facilitating the murders of so many others: "Where political and religious leaders did speak out against the Nazis, notably in . . . Denmark, most Jews were saved. Those Jews who died . . . were victims of the silence of Europe's moral leadership as [much as] they were victims of the Nazis."

While our society still faces serious challenges in remedying hatefulness and discrimination, the specific problems that were so salient for the influential early advocates of non-emergency hate speech restrictions noted above—the dearth of attention to and support for targets of such speech—are now no longer operative. Hateful, discriminatory expressions and actions now not only receive intense media attention, but they are also swiftly and strongly condemned by government officials, community leaders, social media campaigns, and members of the disparaged groups and organizations that champion their rights.

Experts have observed that counterspeech (as well as other antidiscrimination measures) have been so successful that any speech that is even arguably biased has already been pre-emptively discredited at the moment it is uttered—that is, not requiring any specific counterspeech in rebuttal. Indeed, in our contemporary culture, terms such as "racist" and "transphobe" have become some of the most stigmatizing epithets. Two British scholars, Dennis J. Baker and Lucy Zhao, observed that if anyone is marginalized by hateful, discriminatory speech these days, it is those who express hateful opinions, noting that "the message that we are all equal . . . is very visible in Western democracies [and] . . . is backed up with a mass of . . . laws." As a consequence, they concluded, "media scrutiny, public shaming, and strong majority attitudes" should "prevent denigrating expression from making those denigrated feel as less than full members of society." Susan Benesch, the founding director of the Dangerous Speech Project, asks two rhetorical questions to memorably illustrate the relative power of, respectively, (1) the social norms that are both reflected in and reinforced by counterspeech; and (2) government censorship/ punishment: "How many people use the N-word?" and "How many people commit murder or rape?"

Given the troubling ongoing reality of hateful and discriminatory attitudes, expressions, and actions, I am hardly concluding that these problems have disappeared, or that we should not continue to do our utmost to reduce them. Nor am I minimizing the ongoing power of hate speech to inflict psychic and other damage. Rather, I am pointing out that the substantial attention and criticism that these problems now receive, thanks to counterspeech, should diminish hate speech's negative toll according to many experts, including even the original proponents of non-emergency hate speech restrictions in the United States.

Isn't it unrealistic to rely on counterspeech as the primary check against the potentially harmful impact of controversial speech, such as hate speech or misinformation?

There is another common misconception about the role of counterspeech in redressing the potential harms of hate speech: that counterspeech is expected to serve as the primary, or even only, check on hateful, discriminatory attitudes and actions. To the contrary, essential tools include laws against hateful, discriminatory actions, including violence. An enormous body of social science research demonstrates that such laws reduce not only discriminatory conduct, but also discriminatory attitudes.

Initially laid out by Harvard psychology professor Gordon Allport in his classic 1954 book *The Nature of Prejudice*, the "contact theory" posits that the most effective way for people to overcome their prejudice toward someone they view as "other" is to interact with "others." This theory has subsequently been reaffirmed in hundreds of studies. A 2011 meta-analysis of 515 studies, involving more than 250,000 subjects, concluded that "intergroup contact typically reduced prejudice" toward multiple often-stigmatized groups, including various ethnic groups, the disabled, mentally ill people, and LGBTQ+ people. In 2002, a political scientist demonstrated that contact with people who had different political beliefs fostered political tolerance. Social scientists have concluded that this "wide applicability suggests that contact effects may" result from "mere exposure." Experiments have repeatedly shown that greater exposure to members of any "outgroups," standing alone, "can significantly enhance liking for" not only those groups, but also other outgroups. Additionally, these positive results reveal "a remarkable universality," with decreased prejudice manifested "across national, gender, and age groups."

The positive impacts of contact flow not only from the direct contact and communications with actual "others" that result from antidiscrimination and pro-integration measures, but also from the vicarious contact that results from viewing media depictions of such others. While some research indicates that the changed attitudes resulting from vicarious contact might not be as durable as those resulting from actual contact, such vicarious contact is especially beneficial for people who have less opportunity for direct contact with "others."

How effective is counterspeech in comparison to censorship?

The pertinent question about counterspeech is not how effective it is in the abstract, but rather how effective it is compared to censorship—that is, non-emergency speech restrictions. Of course, counterspeech does not completely eliminate the potential adverse impact of problematic speech, but neither does censorship. In fact, experts have concluded that censoring any controversial speech is less effective than counterspeech, and may actually do more harm than good. For instance, multiple human rights activists in many countries and in international agencies have reached this conclusion about hate speech. Even though censoring hate speech is legally permitted in these other countries, many human rights experts have concluded that counterspeech is preferable from a pragmatic perspective. For example, the committee that enforces the UN's International Convention on the Elimination of All Forms of Racial Discrimination (CERD), which requires ratifying countries to outlaw hate speech, in 2013 downplayed censorship and instead stressed the importance of "education for tolerance, and counterspeech . . . [as] effective antidotes to racist hate speech."

Parallel conclusions have been reached by experts who have been studying disinformation and its potential adverse impacts on everything from public health to democracy. Multiple studies have reached a consensus that the most fruitful way to curb disinformation's negative potential impact is to deploy information that can check its spread and influence: targeted responses to specific disinformation; and preemptive general educational approaches, which enhance critical media and information literacy skills. Psychological research shows that even more effective than debunking disinformation after its dissemination is "pre-bunking": inoculating people against disinformation before they are exposed to it. An academic article that was published in August 2022 by researchers at the University of Cambridge, the University of Bristol, and Google detailed seven pre-bunking experiments involving one million adults, and found an increase in their ability to recognize misinformation techniques "not just across the conspiratorial spectrum but across the political spectrum."

Experience has shown that even the most censorial regime will never be able to completely eliminate the supply of controversial speech; some such speech will be driven underground, and some will be camouflaged in more subtle language to elude censors. Given the inevitable, persistent supply of controversial speech, we must focus on reducing the demand for it (i.e., persuading people not to heed it), another essential form of counterspeech. Yes, it's true that counterspeech isn't guaranteed to succeed in suppressing any targeted ideas or expression. But it's also true that censorship is guaranteed to fail in doing so.

11. Shouldn't government have more power to restrict social media because of its unprecedented power to convey harmful speech?

The constant recent calls to restrict expression on social media parallel constant calls, throughout history, to restrict expression on other media that were new at the time. All such advocacy results from the new medium's increased power to transmit expression, including expression feared to have a harmful impact, to a broader audience. For example, the 1525 tirade by the Dutch philosopher Erasmus against the then-newest communications technology—the printing press— foreshadows the current condemnations of social media companies; he complained that the new technology was able to "fill the world with" materials that are "foolish, ignorant, malignant, libellous, mad, impious and subversive; and such is the flood that even things that might have done some good lose all their goodness." With 20/20 hindsight, though, we have repeatedly realized that the potential dangers of new media tend to be exaggerated. Moreover, these potential dangers can be averted, while the new media's positive potential can be maximized, by enforcing the same fundamental free speech standards that apply to older media.

In its landmark 1997 decision in *Reno v. ACLU*, the Supreme Court unanimously rejected arguments that online expression, which was then new and widely feared, should receive anything less than full-fledged First Amendment protection. Likewise, in 2017, the Court struck down restrictions on assertedly dangerous expression on social media, hailing it as "the most important" forum "for the exchange of views." Social media indeed facilitate unparalleled opportunities for unprecedented numbers of people to convey and receive communications—including people whose voices have been marginalized and muted in older media, with their centralized gatekeepers and exponentially higher costs. Consider the grassroots movements that have effectively harnessed social media, including Black Lives Matter and #MeToo. If speech on social media were subject to non-emergency restrictions, the expression of such groups would be especially vulnerable, because such discretionary power is consistently wielded disproportionately against critics of the status quo.

Those who exercise power in any society have generally been hostile toward new media that make it easier, cheaper, and faster for more people to directly access information and ideas. To again quote the old adage: "Knowledge is power." Accordingly, more widely distributing information is tantamount to more widely distributing power. Powerful established media in every era disseminate critiques of the alleged dangers of their newer (and successful) competitors, purportedly due to concern about the public interest, but without acknowledging their conflicting private interests. Today's TV and print journalists relentlessly assail social media—just as newspapers in earlier eras assailed TV, radio, and even the phonograph, citing some of the very same asserted dangers. For example, today's complaints that social media's addictive qualities deprive young people of sleep echo the same complaint about radio when it was new. A typical newspaper story in 1926 lamented that radio was "keeping children . . . up late nights, wearing down their vitality for lack of sleep and making laggards out of them at school."

All new communications media have been greeted with censorial efforts, even in the United States, despite our First Amendment free speech guarantee. Whatever speech topics are considered to be especially dangerous at the time that a new medium becomes available—which in turn reflects whatever societal threats are then widely considered the most dangerous—there is a consistent concern that expression about those topics will be more easily disseminated. Censorship efforts also focus on potential audience members who are considered the most vulnerable to the feared speech; therefore, minors have often borne the brunt of censorship efforts. For example, in the 1950s, when comic books were increasingly popular among young people, there was a mounting concern about what was then called "juvenile delinquency"; not surprisingly, comic books depicting violence or crime were blamed for contributing to this problem, and consequently laws banned their sale to minors.

Fast-forward to the early 1990s, when the general public became aware of the internet. Our nation was then undergoing what has been called a "moral panic" about child sexual exploitation, involving too many exaggerated or even fabricated claims. Of course, *any* sexual (or other) exploitation of a child (or anyone else) is a serious problem, but the magnitude of the problem was overblown, leading to overblown policy responses. In this climate, the internet was feared as potentially facilitating the sexual exploitation of children, prompting Congress to enact the 1996 "Communications Decency Act," which outlawed all "indecent" or "patently offensive" online expression that minors could access—including a vast array of material with positive benefits for minors' well-being, health, and even lives, such as information about sexual orientation, gender identity, contraception, and preventing sexually transmitted diseases. (Online expression that constituted sexual solicitation of a minor—along with such expression in any media—was appropriately criminalized, consistent with the emergency principle.)

In our current era, when social media platforms have become dominant, the three types of controversial speech that have most often been targeted for suppression, mirroring major societal concerns, are hate speech, disinformation, and extremist speech. In consequence, calls for regulating social media usually focus on these kinds of expression.

Regardless of the different factual details in each historical period, there is a common general pattern. Advocates of reining in each new medium stress its harmful potential, losing sight of its positive potential and of non-censorial measures for addressing the feared harm. History has demonstrated the wisdom of continuing to enforce the emergency test/strict scrutiny for speech restrictions in each situation: Government may restrict speech (in any medium) when it can demonstrate that the restriction is necessary and narrowly tailored to promote an important public interest goal, such as children's safety. If the government could further its goal through other means, which are less speech-restrictive, then the government must do so.

When the Supreme Court examined the Communications Decency Act's censorious provisions regarding online speech in 1997, it unanimously concluded that the indisputably important goal of protecting children's safety could be advanced at least as effectively through more narrowly tailored, less speech-restrictive measures, which would not suppress adults' free speech rights. The Court noted that individual parents could choose to install filtering and blocking software on their own home computers, to shield their own young children from certain online material.

Recent government actions that restrict additional speech on social media—beyond what may be restricted under the emergency/strict scrutiny tests—reflect the consistent general pattern for such non-emergency speech restrictions: Enforcing officials exercise their discretion to suppress views that they disfavor. For example, key officials in the Biden administration, as well as Democratic members of Congress, have strongly pressured social media companies to restrict expression that is inconsistent with the administration's preferred policies on important controverted issues, including elections and COVID. Correspondingly, state laws that Republican lawmakers have enacted require social media companies to host certain conservative content.

Both forms of official compulsion not only contravene free speech values, limiting the expressive choices of platforms and their users; such compulsion also subverts the very values that prompt the speech restrictions. While the advocates of these restrictions tout the important goals of countering disinformation and promoting democracy, in fact, the restrictions hamper democratic self-governance and the search for truth, both of which depend on the most vigorous exchanges among "We the People," free from government censorship. As Justice Robert Jackson wrote in 1945: "The very purpose of the First Amendment is to foreclose public authority from assuming a guardianship of the public mind . . . . [E]very person must be his own watchman for truth, because the forefathers did not trust any government to separate the true from the false for us."

12. Don't social media algorithms warrant more government restrictions because they manipulate people into "echo chambers" and "rabbit holes," thus undermining both liberty and democracy?

Expression on social media—along with expression on all media—may contribute to serious problems, including polarization. Many politicians and commentators blame online platforms for polarization. However, these critics have not made an evidence-based case that such platforms' net impact on polarization is negative, given their provision of fact-checking and other resources that can well reduce polarization. Nor have critics of social media shown that it has a greater impact than other media in fueling polarization. Correspondingly, these critics have not shown that government regulation of social media expression would materially reduce polarization, much less that it would do so more effectively than non-censorial strategies, including measures facilitating users' informed choices about which online expression to view and to credit.

Does evidence show that social media fuel polarization?

In our ongoing "techlash," the giant platforms have become the scapegoats for too many problems for too many people, who accordingly advocate censoring online expression as the purported quick fix. For example, notwithstanding their vast policy differences during the 2020 election campaign—including their diametrically different views about what was (allegedly) wrong with online expression—both Donald Trump and Joe Biden concurred that online platforms should lose their immunity for third-party content under the 1996 federal law known as "Section 230."

The tech giants wield enormous power over our communications—and hence over our freedom of speech, as well as our democratic self-government. Accordingly, platforms' actions warrant critical scrutiny, so we can design well-tailored policy responses. That is precisely why we must avoid jumping to conclusions that aren't sufficiently grounded in evidence and analysis. Throughout history, controversial expression on new media has been blamed for the then-current societal problems, leading to censorship that turns out to be the worst of both worlds: It stifles free speech but does not meaningfully address the pertinent problems.

Following the prevalent historical pattern, too many current critics of polarization conclusorily scapegoat social media communications as bearing the brunt of the blame, without sufficient analysis. First Amendment law sensibly provides that speech should be restricted only as a last resort, when evidence shows that the restriction would materially advance the goal at issue, and that non-censorial measures can't effectively do so. After all, it doesn't make sense to censor speech in order to reduce polarization, if the censorship doesn't actually reduce polarization, or if non-censorial strategies would do so as effectively.

Evidence indicates that polarization is fueled by multiple factors, including expression on traditional media, and that online media may not even have a net negative impact in this regard. Along with social media, traditional media also seek engagement by playing to audience members' anger and fear, as underscored by the old adage, "If it bleeds, it leads." Also parallel to social media, traditional media have courted particular audience segments in terms of partisan affiliations and ideological beliefs. Moreover, there are indications that even mainstream media, which formerly sought to appeal to broader audiences, are now instead cultivating niche audiences, and feeding them content that appeals to and deepens their ideological allegiances. Just as the "surveillance capitalism" business model of social media has allegedly driven the "echo chamber" phenomenon, the new subscriber-based business model of formerly ad-dependent traditional media has allegedly had a parallel impact.

Studies by reputable scholars have concluded that people who gain their information online typically consult more sources, with more diverse perspectives, than people who gain their information through legacy media. Additionally, online platforms facilitate fact-checking and other research, which counters the potential negative impact of misleading or biased communications. These considerations certainly do not suggest that we should overlook problems of online disinformation and polarization, but rather that we should not exaggerate them at the cost of insufficiently addressing other significant contributors to these problems.

How can we facilitate online users' autonomy?

In order to rationally assess the impact of the tech giants' content curating practices, and to design appropriate policy responses, we must obtain sufficient information about these practices. Credible sources have cited evidence that the companies are engaging in unprecedentedly pervasive and granular surveillance of our online activities, and then using the resulting detailed information, with the aid of algorithms, to present each of us with individualized content streams that are designed to prolong our engagement, including by stimulating negative emotions. As noted above, legacy media have similar economic incentives to prolong audience engagement, in light of the subscriber-based business models that they have adopted, now that their social media competitors have cornered the advertising market. Nonetheless, the online media may well be engaging in data surveillance and curation practices that violate individuals' freedom of choice at such a vastly increased scale, and with such reduced notice and consent, as to warrant special consumer protection measures.

Even the platforms' customers do not receive meaningful notice of the companies' practices concerning the data that the customers both provide and receive, let alone consent to these practices. The data of the platforms' non-customers are reportedly also subject to surveillance, as to which they receive no notice, and provide no consent, at all.

Some commentators charge that the Big Tech platforms manipulate users in ways of which the users are unaware. Others respond that these charges are overblown, and that they recycle similarly overblown charges about other media when they were new. For example, in 1957, when TVs were becoming common in homes throughout the United States, journalist Vance Packard's bestselling book *The Hidden Persuaders* maintained that TV ads used subliminal messaging to manipulate viewers to favor particular products and politicians. A 2013 re-examination of this book in the *Journal of Advertising* rejected these charges. Perhaps a future re-examination of today's claims about social media's manipulative power will reach similar conclusions.

Even if Big Tech's "design choices" do in fact "interfere with the free choices of users," as stated in proposed Congressional legislation that would mandate various content curation practices, any top-down, one-size-fits-all federal control also interferes with users' choices.

Regardless of what the tech platforms' data practices and their impacts might actually be, the platforms should greatly increase the transparency of these practices, for the benefit of both individual users and policymakers. The platforms should provide aggregate data to pertinent academic researchers and government bodies—for example, agencies that protect consumer privacy.

Moreover, policymakers should seriously consider requiring meaningful disclosure and opt-in consent before platforms may collect customer data, or curate the content customers receive. After all, freedom of speech entails the right to make one's own choices about what information and ideas to receive—and not to receive. To be sure, the First Amendment does not directly constrain online platforms, because they are private sector entities. Nonetheless, given the platforms' enormous power over the political speech that is the lifeblood of our democracy, free speech should be protected for platforms' customers (and non-customers) through other means, including potentially through the suggested consumer protection and privacy regulations.

To further facilitate meaningful freedom of choice for platform users, another policy proposal that bears serious consideration is requiring the platforms to offer users a range of filtering options both directly and by enabling other software providers to "interoperate" with the platforms' key elements.

Such measures could potentially enable users to choose the types of content they do not wish to receive (if any), criteria for determining the order of their content feed, and their preferred privacy settings. In contrast with direct government regulations of platforms' content curation practices, which in turn constrain users' content choices, regulations that promote users' informed options are consistent with free speech concerns.

While empowering platform users to make their own choices about what online communications they will or will not see is positive from a free speech perspective, it is a double-edged sword in terms of users' exposure to disinformation and other potentially polarizing expression. Some users will opt for diverse perspectives and fact-checking authorities, but others will embrace the opportunity to view increasingly narrow and extreme perspectives on both ends of the political spectrum.

Even the most censorial regime could not completely suppress the supply of problematic expression, which means that the most promising countermeasures focus on reducing the demand for it. Therefore, from the earliest ages on, we must all learn the values and civic virtues that undergird our pluralistic democracy, as well as information literacy and critical reading skills, so that we will be less likely to seek out potentially problematic material, or to be negatively influenced by it.

3

FREE SPEECH RIGHTS THAT THE FIRST AMENDMENT PROTECTS

What is First Amendment law?

This body of law consists of the U.S. Supreme Court decisions that interpret and apply the First Amendment in the context of particular cases (i.e., lawsuits) that the Court reviews. Along with all constitutional law, First Amendment law is a type of "common law" or "case law," which develops incrementally over time, in a case-by-case manner. This type of law contrasts with statutory law, which comprehensively spells out the detailed rules governing the issues that the statute addresses.

What is protected "freedom of speech" under the First Amendment?

I will answer this important overarching question by breaking it down into the multiple more specific subquestions it encompasses. Before doing so, however, I will sketch out the overall framework of the Court's answers to the overarching question.

The Court has determined the scope of First Amendment speech protection in cases deciding whether various government regulations violate that freedom. Each case presents two major questions. The first is whether the regulated expressive conduct[1] constitutes "speech" within the scope of the Free

Speech Clause, so that it is entitled to some constitutional protection. A current important issue about the contours of "speech" within the First Amendment concerns social media platforms' content moderation policies. Some judges have ruled that these policies are analogous to newspapers' editorial policies, and hence come within the Free Speech Clause's ambit, while other judges have rejected that argument, and the Supreme Court has not yet (as of May 2023) addressed the issue.

Even if the Court decides that the regulated expression or conduct in a particular case constitutes "speech" that is entitled to some First Amendment protection, the regulation isn't necessarily unconstitutional. First Amendment law doesn't deem freedom of speech to be absolute, but rather permits the government to restrict speech in accordance with specified rules and standards. Therefore, the second major question in every free speech case is whether the challenged speech regulation is permissible or not. To be sure, government has less latitude to regulate speech (or other fundamental rights) than it does to regulate other matters. Nonetheless, as answers throughout this book illustrate, the Court has upheld many speech restrictions.

What does the First Amendment's Free Speech Clause provide?

The First Amendment's "Free Speech Clause" provides: "Congress shall make no law . . . abridging the freedom of speech." Although this language might seem quite specific, every key word in it has been vigorously debated, and subject to differing interpretations by Supreme Court Justices and other experts.

How does the Supreme Court interpret the First Amendment's language?

In general, the modern Court—starting in the second half of the 20th century—has construed this language expansively, including by treating it as setting out broad general principles that apply to current situations and new communications technologies, which did not exist when the Amendment was adopted in 1791. This flexible construction of the First Amendment, extending it to evolving forms of communications, was embraced even by Justice Antonin Scalia, the Court's leading champion of "originalism" (i.e., interpreting the Constitution in accordance with its "original public meaning" in 1791). In his historic 2008 opinion that expansively interpreted the Second Amendment "right to bear arms," Scalia made this important point about the First Amendment:

> Some have made the argument, bordering on the frivolous, that only those arms in existence in the 18th century are protected by the Second Amendment. We do not interpret constitutional rights that way. *Just as the First Amendment protects modern forms of communications . . .,* the Second Amendment extends . . . to all . . . bearable arms, even those that were not in existence at the time of the founding. [emphasis added]

The next series of questions and answers will chronicle how the modern Court has interpreted the most important words and phrases in the Free Speech Clause. By way of preview, the bold language immediately below sets out a clarified, expanded version of this constitutional language, which summarizes the Court's major interpretations; the clause's actual words are bracketed in italics after the pertinent portion of the clarified version:

No government official or agency [*Congress*] **may take any action** [*shall make no law*] **that substantially limits or deters** [*abridging*] **any expression or expressive conduct** [*the freedom of speech*] **unless the government demonstrates that the action is justified under the**

applicable legal test; in many cases, the applicable test requires the government to show that the action substantially promotes a very important public purpose and is necessary (i.e., the least speech-restrictive alternative option) for doing so. In exceptional situations, the same limits apply to actions by private sector actors: when they are carrying out a function that traditionally, exclusively has been carried out by the government; or when they are sufficiently "entangled" with the government, such as when they are acting under coercive government pressure or in close collaboration with the government.

How does the Court interpret "Congress" and "law"?

The Court has construed "Congress" to refer not only to the sole government body to which that word literally refers—the legislative branch of the national government—but also to all government bodies and officials, in all branches and levels of government in the United States, ranging from local police officers and schoolteachers[2] to the president of the United States. In parallel fashion, the Court has construed the word "law" to encompass not only the legislation or regulations to which it literally refers, but also any other official action undertaken by any government agent or body.

While the Free Speech Clause encompasses all governmental actions, it generally does not encompass any non-government action; with only two narrow exceptions, the Clause does not extend to any private sector action. The legal term for this important concept is "the state action doctrine," signaling that the First Amendment (as well as almost all other rights-securing constitutional provisions) applies only to "state" action, with the term "state" referring to government generally. Consistent with this doctrine, if a public university bars its students from criticizing its policies, the students may claim that their First Amendment rights have been violated. In contrast, if a private university bars its students from criticizing its policies, the students have no First Amendment claim. (As a later answer explains, they may well have other legal claims, however.)

There are two limited exceptions to the state action doctrine, which subject certain private sector actions to First Amendment (as well as other constitutional) constraints. First, the "public function" exception applies when the private actor performs a function that has "traditionally exclusively" been performed by the government. On this rationale, for example, private prisons may be required to respect inmates' First Amendment rights to the same extent as government prisons. In contrast, courts have ruled that this exception does not extend to social media companies because the provision of communications platforms is not a function that government has "traditionally *exclusively*" performed; many private sector entities also have provided such platforms.

The second exception to the state action doctrine is the "entanglement" exception. It applies when the private sector actor is closely "entangled" with the government, including when the government coerces it to carry out the action in question or acts in close coordination with the private sector entity. As I am completing this book (in May 2023), many lawsuits are pending in which people whose speech has been restricted on private online platforms—such as Facebook, Twitter, and YouTube—contend that the entanglement exception applies to their situations. The plaintiffs maintain, for instance, that government officials threatened (implicitly, if not explicitly) to impose punitive measures on these tech companies (e.g., subjecting them to antitrust enforcement) if they did not restrict certain "disinformation" about matters such as COVID or elections. The Supreme Court has not yet weighed in on any of these cases.

How does the Court interpret "abridging"?

The First Amendment religious liberty clause bars any "law . . . *prohibiting* the free exercise" of religion, in contrast to the freedom of speech and press clauses, which bar any "law . . . *abridging* the freedom of speech, or of the press." Accordingly, the First Amendment's explicit language bars not only such outright "prohibitions" on free expression as criminal bans or prior restraints, but also other measures that "abridge" or limit free expression. The Supreme Court consistently has held that the Free Speech Clause is implicated by any government measure that, as a practical matter, substantially curtails free expression, including by exerting a sufficient deterrent or "chilling" impact on it.

Let me describe an important case that implemented this functional concept of "abridgement." In 1963 the Court held that the First Amendment was violated by notices that a Rhode Island government commission sent to distributors of books and magazines indicating that some publications they distributed could be subject to prosecution as illegal obscenity. Even though the commission had no power to institute obscenity prosecutions, the Court concluded that its notices had the effect of intimidating distributors, who therefore were likely to cease distributing the works in question even absent prosecution. Specifically, the notices advised the distributors that the commission had a duty to recommend prosecution of "purveyors of obscenity," and that it had circulated lists of "objectionable" publications to local police departments; the notices also requested the distributors' "cooperation." The Court commented that it would "look through forms to the substance and recognize that informal censorship may sufficiently inhibit the circulation of publications to warrant" First Amendment protection.

The Court has deemed a wide range of government actions to have sufficiently speech-suppressive impacts to constitute "abridgements" of speech that warrant First Amendment review. For example, the Court has struck down laws that limited the ability of certain individuals—including government employees and people convicted of crimes—to be paid for certain writings they authored, reasoning that the denial of payment would deter the writing; indeed, that was precisely the purpose of the payment bans.

How does the Court interpret "No law . . . abridging the freedom of speech"?

Former Supreme Court Justice Hugo Black, who generally espoused speech-protective views about the Free Speech Clause, repeatedly stressed that the Clause's word "no" should be construed literally, as permitting no "law . . . abridging the freedom of speech" whatsoever. Along with all other strong free speech proponents, however, Black did support some speech-restricting measures; he justified this position by construing such measures as not in fact "abridging the freedom of speech," specifically because he read the term "speech" as literally as he read the term "no." In contrast with other modern-era Justices, Black concluded that "speech" did not extend to nonverbal expressive conduct such as labor picketing and wearing black armbands.

Other free speech proponents, including Justices, have endorsed certain speech restrictions on the ground that they do not "abridge" or violate "the freedom of speech," reasoning that this freedom does not extend to speech that poses an emergency. The best-known statement of this view was in a much-quoted 1919 opinion by Justice Oliver Wendell Holmes: "The most stringent protection of free speech would not protect a man falsely shouting fire in a theatre and causing a panic."

In short, the word "no" cannot be read in isolation, but only in conjunction with the phrase to which it refers: "law . . . abridging the freedom of speech." There is a consensus that some speech restrictions do not constitute the forbidden type of law, although there continues to be much debate about whether particular restrictions are forbidden or not.

How does the Court interpret "speech"?

Before answering this specific question, I want to remind readers of the limited—even though important—role it plays in the overall First Amendment analysis. Even if the Court agreed that a challenged regulation targeted "speech," the Court could still uphold the regulation. To quote the Free Speech Clause's language, a restriction on "speech" does not necessarily constitute a "law . . . abridging the freedom of speech." In other words, for a speech restriction to violate the First Amendment, it is necessary—but not sufficient—that the restriction limits expressive conduct that is considered "speech."

All modern Justices have expansively interpreted "speech" as designating much more than its most literal meaning, which denotes "talking." Rather, the modern Court has consistently treated "speech" as synonymous with "expression" of any mode, including not only words but also images. Additionally, the modern Court has broadly construed "speech" as including expression that is conveyed via any means of communication.[3] As the Court declared in a 2010 decision involving video games: "[T]he basic principles of freedom of speech and the press do not vary when a new and different medium for communication appears." That said, consistent with the Court's fact-specific application of general First Amendment principles, it has held that the Free Speech Clause does not necessarily apply identically in the context of various communications technologies. Most importantly, certain "patently offensive" or "indecent" expression that is constitutionally protected in all other media—including certain four-letter words—is unprotected in over-the-air radio and TV broadcasts.

The Court has expansively interpreted "speech" in yet another respect—as extending to certain nonverbal expression, which it sometimes labels "symbolic expression," "symbolic conduct," or "expressive conduct." Classic examples include wearing an armband, burning a U.S. flag, and marching in a demonstration. On the one hand, the Court has rejected "the view that an apparently limitless variety of conduct can be labeled 'speech' whenever the person engaging in the conduct intends thereby to express an idea." On the other hand, it has recognized that "a narrow, succinctly articulable message is not" a prerequisite for First Amendment protection, observing that such a standard would exclude "the unquestionably shielded painting of Jackson Pollock, music of Arnold Schoenberg, or Jabberwocky verse of Lewis Carroll." The Court has thus held that marches or parades constitute protected expression because they have an "inherent expressiveness," even when "combining multifarious voices" that do not "isolate an exact message."

The foregoing discussion demonstrates that it is not true—contrary to common pronouncements—that the First Amendment protects speech, but not conduct. Rather, whether the First Amendment protects particular expression from particular restrictions depends not on whether the expression might be labeled "speech" versus "conduct" (which, after all, are not clear-cut, categorical distinctions), but rather on whether the restriction satisfies the applicable standards for assessing whether it constitutes an impermissible "abridgement" of expression. Because these standards are fact-specific, requiring evaluation of all the pertinent facts and circumstances, the very same expression—including expressive conduct—could permissibly be restricted in one context, but not in another. For example, the government may punish someone who burned a flag on a public street without complying with environmental and safety limits that apply to all fires on public streets, even if the flag burning was intended to and did convey a protest message. In contrast, if the flag burning did comply with applicable environmental and safety limits, but was nonetheless punished (whereas comparable fires, which burned leaves, were not), that would violate the First Amendment. The critical issue is whether the government is punishing the message that the expressive conduct conveys—which would violate the cardinal viewpoint-neutrality principle—or whether the government is, rather, enforcing viewpoint-neutral rules that promote important public purposes, such as public health and safety.

Let me cite one important example of expressive conduct that the Court held to be protected in a noteworthy 1963 case: litigation for the purpose of advancing racial justice (and other public interest causes). The Court upheld the rights of the NAACP and NAACP Legal Defense and Educational Fund to engage in litigation as "a means for achieving the . . . equality of treatment for" Black people. The Court elaborated: "Groups which find themselves unable to achieve their objectives through the ballot frequently turn to the courts. . . . [L]itigation may well be the sole practicable avenue open to a minority to petition for redress of grievances." For these reasons, the Court concluded that the NAACP litigation was a "form of political expression" and struck down a 1956 Virginia statute that broadly banned attorneys' solicitation of clients, which state officials had enforced to bar NAACP lawsuits. Indeed, Justice William O. Douglas's concurring opinion cited evidence that the statute had been enacted precisely for purposes of thwarting the NAACP's school desegregation litigation in the wake of the Court's historic 1954 and 1955 *Brown v. Board of Education* rulings.

Has the Court held that "money is speech"?

In a series of decisions dating back to its 1976 *Buckley v. Valeo* ruling, the Supreme Court has held that the First Amendment governs restrictions on "campaign finance": making financial contributions to, or spending money on behalf of, political campaigns for candidates or ballot issues. The Court has held that spending money to advance a political message constitutes expressive conduct, just as it has held regarding a wide array of other conduct that advances political messages (e.g., burning a flag, wearing an armband, marching in a parade, and pursuing litigation). Also mirroring its holdings in myriad other expressive conduct cases, the Court has held that when the government's regulation of political spending targets the expressive aspect of this conduct, that regulation implicates First Amendment rights. To again invoke the flag burning analogy, when a government restriction singles out expressive flag burning, rather than the burning of objects in general, that restriction implicates First Amendment rights and therefore must survive First Amendment scrutiny. Likewise, First Amendment review is also triggered by government restrictions that focus not on spending money in general, but rather on spending money to advance political messages.

In *Buckley*, the Court explained how the "contribution and expenditure limitations" in campaign finance laws curtail expression because they "impose direct quantity restrictions on political communication and association by persons, groups, candidates, and political parties":

> A restriction on the amount of money a person or group can spend on political communication . . . necessarily reduces the quantity of expression by restricting the number of issues discussed, the depth of their exploration, and the size of the audience reached. This is because virtually every means of communicating ideas . . . requires the expenditure of money. The distribution of the humblest handbill or leaflet entails printing, paper, and circulation costs. Speeches and rallies generally necessitate hiring a hall and publicizing the event. The electorate's increasing dependence on . . . mass media . . . has made these expensive modes of communication indispensable instruments of effective political speech.

As earlier answers have explained, the fact that a government restriction implicates First Amendment rights does not mean that the restriction is automatically unconstitutional. To the contrary, many restrictions on First Amendment rights are held not to constitute unconstitutional "abridgements" of "the freedom of speech." Accordingly, the Court has rejected First Amendment challenges to multiple campaign finance restrictions. For example, even in the controversial 2010 *Citizens United* decision, which upheld the First Amendment challenge to some campaign finance restrictions on unions and corporations (including non-profit corporations), the Court also rejected the First Amendment challenge to other such restrictions.

The preceding summary of the Court's campaign finance rulings should make clear that, contrary to the rhetoric that critics of these rulings commonly deploy, the Court never has supported the plainly nonsensical holding that "money is speech." Rather, consistent with its long line of expressive conduct cases concerning widely diverse conduct, the campaign finance decisions have supported two other holdings that are plainly sensible: first, that the conduct of spending money in the campaign context is intended to and does in fact convey messages; and second, that restrictions on this expressive conduct have the impact of restricting the messages.

Underscoring the common-sense nature of these actual holdings is the fact that they have been supported by all but one of the many, ideologically diverse Justices who have ruled on these issues since 1976.[4] Likewise, all but one of these Justices have agreed that campaign finance regulations should be subject to rigorous First Amendment scrutiny, with the government bearing the burden of showing that the regulations significantly promote substantial public interests and are narrowly tailored to do so. To be sure, the Justices have strongly disagreed about whether the government satisfied this burden of proof concerning particular regulations.

In sum, the Court has never said that "money is speech," but—with almost unanimous support among all Justices from 1976 onward—it has recognized that spending money facilitates the exercise of speech freedom, while restricting such spending does the opposite.

What is the relationship between "freedom of speech" and other, similar rights that the First Amendment also explicitly protects?

In addition to the Free Speech Clause, the First Amendment contains five other clauses, two of which concern religion,[5] and three of which are closely related to speech: "Congress shall make no law . . . abridging the freedom of speech, or of the *press*; or the right of the People peaceably to *assemble*, and to *petition* the Government for a redress of grievances" [emphasis added]. These other clauses refer to particular modes of expression, and therefore they have been assimilated into the Court's broad construction of the concept of "speech," which itself extends to all modes of expression, including via the "press," "assembly," and/or "petition." Consequently, the same general First Amendment principles and standards that the Court has forged to assess the constitutionality of restrictions on "speech" also govern restrictions on the specific, important types of expression these other clauses single out.

What is the relationship between "freedom of speech" and "freedom of the press"?

One key question about the relationships among the Free Speech Clause and other First Amendment clauses concerns the relationship between the speech and press clauses in particular: By virtue of the latter clause, should members of "the press" (i.e., institutional media and professional journalists) receive any additional protections, beyond those that the Free Speech Clause secures for all members of the general public? It has been argued that the Free Press Clause extends two special First Amendment rights to professional journalists, but not to members of the general public.

First, it has been argued that journalists should have special rights of access to certain government institutions or activities that are off-limits to members of the general public (e.g., prisons or military operations). Given the public's significant First Amendment interest in receiving information about the pertinent government institutions and actions, the argument goes, members of the institutional press should have special rights of access, acting on behalf of the general public. Various government agencies and officials have chosen to offer special rights of access to members of the press. For example, U.S. military officials have permitted members of a "press pool" to obtain special access to military operations. As another example, the Supreme Court has set aside seats in its relatively small courtroom for members of the press.

A second type of special First Amendment right also has been advocated to pertain only to members of "the press": a "reporters' privilege," which insulates journalists from having to disclose their confidential sources even when members of the general public would have to provide comparable information (e.g., when subpoenaed to provide information in grand jury investigations). Advocates of this privilege maintain that it would incentivize people to provide information to reporters, which they would not provide unless the reporters could pledge to maintain confidentiality. Paralleling the rationale for special press access to government institutions and actions, the rationale for a special reporters' privilege is based not only on the journalists' own First Amendment interests, but also on those of the general public; the public would benefit from any information that reporters would be able to gain thanks to the privilege. Just as a number of officials and agencies have chosen to provide members of the press with special access to certain government institutions and actions, almost all state legislatures have chosen to enact "shield laws," guaranteeing the reporters' privilege in specified circumstances.

Although certain government officials and bodies have chosen to provide special rights to some journalists, as described above, the Supreme Court never has held that the First Amendment requires government to protect such special rights. To the contrary, in several cases during the 1970s, the Court consistently rejected journalists' claims that they should have special rights of access to prison facilities. Although these cases happened to involve prisons, the Court's rejection of the press's special access claims was phrased more broadly, apparently rejecting any such claim regarding any government institution or action. For example, in the first such case, the Court sweepingly declared that "[t]he Constitution does not . . . require government to accord to the press special access to information not shared by members of the public generally."

Similarly, the Supreme Court's sole case to consider the claim that the First Amendment guarantees the reporters' privilege, in 1972, rejected that claim. The Court did recognize that the First Amendment provides some protection for the news gathering process, given how essential that process is: "[W]ithout some protection for seeking out the news, freedom of the press could be eviscerated." Nonetheless, the Court concluded that there was inadequate evidence that the news gathering process would be sufficiently hampered by the absence of a reporters' privilege to outweigh the countervailing law enforcement interests. In addition, the Justices noted that it would be difficult to decide who should—and should not—be entitled to exercise such a privilege. The Court observed that freedom of the press has always extended to "the lonely pamphleteer" as well as "the large metropolitan publisher." Furthermore, the Court stressed, "the informative function" that "representatives of the organized press" serve "is also performed by lecturers, political pollsters, novelists, academic researchers, and dramatists." Therefore, the Court rejected the notion that "freedom of the press" confers special rights, above and beyond those secured by "freedom of speech."

These decisions rejecting any special First Amendment rights for journalists are a half-century old, and the Court never has reexamined them or revisited these issues. In the intervening decades, the advent of the internet has further blurred the always-unclear line (if any) between members of "the press" and of the general public, thus further undermining claims that these two groups should have different First Amendment rights.

What speech-related rights has the Supreme Court held to be implicitly protected by the First Amendment?

Even beyond the multiple speech-related rights that the First Amendment expressly protects, the Supreme Court has construed the First Amendment as implicitly protecting additional, closely connected rights. In contrast with some other unenumerated rights that Supreme Court opinions have held to be implicitly protected by other constitutional provisions—notably, the right to choose an abortion under the Fourteenth Amendment's Due Process Clause—the implied First Amendment rights have not been controversial.[6] Instead, these unenumerated First Amendment freedoms have been supported by all modern Justices, all across the ideological spectrum. As the Court stated in a 1982 case: "The First Amendment is . . . broad enough to encompass those rights that, while not unambiguously enumerated in the very terms of the Amendment, are nonetheless necessary to the enjoyment of other First Amendment rights." At least some of these implicit First Amendment freedoms are considered so important, and indeed so widely taken for granted, that many people are surprised to learn that they are not explicitly set out in that Amendment (or elsewhere in the Constitution).

I list these implicitly protected First Amendment rights below, with brief explanatory notes about each. One major point that previous answers noted bears repeating in this context: Just as "speech" itself is not immune from all restrictions, the same is true for these implicitly protected First Amendment freedoms.

What is freedom of thought and belief?

Sometimes described as "freedom of conscience," this right extends to both religious beliefs (which are also protected by the First Amendment's Free Exercise Clause) and secular beliefs and ideas.

Freedom of conscience has a mutually reinforcing relationship with freedom of speech. Without freedom of thought, freedom of speech would be meaningless, since individuals would be limited to conveying only officially approved ideas and beliefs. By the same token, though, without freedom of speech, it is difficult to meaningfully exercise one's freedom of thought. As the Supreme Court declared in 2001, "speech is the beginning of thought."

What is the freedom not to speak?

In a landmark 1943 decision, *West Virginia Board of Education v. Barnette*, the Supreme Court for the first time expressly protected both the implied freedom of conscience and the implied freedom from compelled expression. The Court specifically held that both of these unenumerated First Amendment rights were violated by state laws compelling public school students to salute the U.S. flag and recite the Pledge of Allegiance. These laws had been challenged by members of the Jehovah's Witnesses religious denomination, who believed that such salutes constituted idolatry, violating the biblical Second Commandment. The Court could have protected the Witnesses' rights specifically under the First Amendment's Free Exercise Clause, given the religious nature of their beliefs. Instead, though, the Court's rationale reflected broad concerns about freedom of conscience more generally. As the Court elaborated in a later case, "[t]he right to speak and the right to refrain from speaking are complementary components of the broader concept of 'individual freedom of mind.'"

In *Barnette*, the Court indicated that First Amendment freedoms may well be even more endangered by government-coerced expression than by government-coerced silence. In one of the most widely quoted statements the Court has ever issued, it declared:

> If there is any fixed star in our constitutional constellation, it is that no official, high or petty, can prescribe what shall be orthodox in politics, nationalism, religion, or other matters of opinion, or force citizens to confess by word or act their faith therein. If there are any circumstances which permit an exception, they do not now occur to us.

Considering that the mandatory flag salute laws were issued to promote national unity and security when the United States was engaged in World War II, the government's stated purpose was supremely important. Thus it is especially significant that the Court nevertheless held that even this purpose could not legitimate infringing freedom of conscience through compelled speech.

The Court has applied *Barnette*'s principles to many factual situations, including compelled statements of fact, as well as the "matters of opinion" to which *Barnette* expressly referred. Consequently, for example, the Court struck down a state law requirement that professional fundraisers must disclose to potential donors the percentage of charitable contributions collected during the previous year that were actually turned over to charity. However, since "commercial speech" traditionally has received less First Amendment protection than speech with other content, the Court has held that government may require the dissemination of "purely factual and uncontroversial information" in commercial advertising. For instance, in a 1985 case, the Court upheld a requirement that attorneys who solicited clients on a contingent fee basis—whereby clients would only have to pay lawyers' fees if the lawsuit resulted in financial recovery—had to alert prospective clients that they would be responsible for covering certain court costs no matter what the lawsuit's outcome.

Barnette has been cited in many recent discussions concerning the mandatory statements that have been proliferating on our nation's campuses. These include mandatory "DEI" statements on the part of applicants for faculty jobs or promotions, which describe the applicants' work to promote "diversity, equity and inclusion," and mandatory "land acknowledgment" statements on course syllabi, conveying the educational institution's official views about Native American property rights in the land it now occupies. In 2021 and 2022, the nonpartisan, ideologically diverse Academic Freedom Alliance (AFA) urged higher education institutions not to demand any such statements either on course syllabi or as conditions of employment or promotion. Referring to the long-discredited "loyalty oaths" that educational institutions imposed on faculty members during the Cold War/McCarthy period, which the Supreme Court struck down under the First Amendment, the AFA emphasized that the current mandatory statements—although different in content—"are in principle indistinguishable from" any "other statements of belief that university officials have . . . attempted to force members of the faculty to endorse in the past." Consistent with the fundamental viewpoint-neutrality principle, the AFA underscored: "No matter how widely shared or normatively desirable any particular statement of values might be, individual professors should not be . . . coerced to endorse . . . such statements."

What is the freedom to speak anonymously or pseudonymously?

One specific aspect of the freedom not to speak is speakers' freedom not to reveal who they are. Many laws governing the distribution of written materials in connection with political campaigns have required their authors to disclose their identities. In striking down myriad such laws, the

Supreme Court has emphasized that the required disclosure will likely chill speech, especially when the speakers and/ or their perspectives are unpopular. Moreover, even if mandatory disclosure doesn't completely silence speech, such disclosure could well mute the speech's impact. In a 1995 decision, which invalidated a law barring the distribution of anonymous campaign literature, the Court observed that a speaker's decision to remain anonymous "may be motivated by fear of economic or official retaliation [or] social ostracism"; furthermore, the Court observed, anonymity enables a speaker "who may be personally unpopular to ensure that readers will not prejudge her message simply because they do not like its proponent."

What is the right to receive information and ideas?

The Supreme Court has recognized that freedom of speech protects not only a speaker's right to convey information and ideas, but also a listener's right to receive them. One of the earliest expositions of this important implicit First Amendment right came from the great abolitionist orator, Frederick Douglass. He was responding to a situation in 1860, when a pro-slavery mob violently terminated an abolitionist meeting in Boston, which he had been scheduled to address. In Douglass's words: "To suppress free speech is a double wrong. It violates the rights of the hearer as well as those of the speaker."

Of the many Supreme Court opinions that have upheld this implied First Amendment right, I will quote two, both authored by Justice William Brennan, which spell out how it reinforces the right to convey ideas on the part of both speakers and listeners. In a 1965 opinion, Brennan wrote: "The dissemination of ideas can accomplish nothing if otherwise willing addressees are not free to receive and consider them. It would be a barren marketplace of ideas that had only sellers, and no buyers." And in a 1982 opinion, Brennan added: "[T]he right to receive ideas is a necessary predicate to the recipient's meaningful exercise of his own rights of speech."

What is freedom of association?

Contrary to a common misunderstanding, this well-known right is not expressly set out in the Constitution. To be sure, the First Amendment does expressly protect "the right of the people peaceably to assemble," which is one important manifestation of the more general freedom of association. While this explicit "Assembly Clause" focuses on public gatherings, the implied freedom of association extends to meetings in private settings, and even to "intimate associations," such as relationships among family members and friends.

The Court first protected the implied freedom of association in its pathbreaking unanimous 1958 decision in *NAACP v. Alabama*. Multiple Southern states were subjecting the NAACP to various burdensome and punitive measures in an effort to disrupt its campaign against Jim Crow laws. One such measure, which the Court struck down in this case, was the requirement that the NAACP disclose its membership lists. The Court held that this requirement impermissibly burdened the associational freedom of people who would otherwise choose to become or remain NAACP members, given how deeply controversial the organization and its civil rights mission then were in the Deep South, prompting reasonable fears that identified members would face various punitive consequences.

Such reasonable fears underscore the importance of not only freedom of association, but also the closely interrelated right to speak anonymously, as prerequisites for the actual exercise of speech rights. Because individuals might well be afraid to speak up on behalf of unpopular causes, it is essential that they have the right to do so anonymously, and to amplify their individual voices by banding together with other like-minded people, while maintaining their anonymity. As the Supreme Court declared in the *NAACP v. Alabama* case: "Effective advocacy of . . . points of view, particularly controversial ones, is undeniably enhanced by group association. . . . [Such] freedom . . . is an inseparable aspect of . . . freedom of speech."

What types of groups are protected by freedom of association?

The Supreme Court has protected freedom of association for both "intimate" and "expressive" associations. As the label suggests, intimate associations constitute relatively small groups and are based on personal relationships, including family ties. Expressive associations include large groups of people who band together for a range of purposes, including expressive purposes. (From now on, this book's references to freedom of association designate this expressive type of association.)

The Supreme Court's seminal 1958 *NAACP v. Alabama* case stressed that the freedom of association, along with freedom of speech itself, applies to all ideas, regardless of subject or viewpoint: "[I]t is immaterial whether the beliefs sought to be advanced by association pertain to political, economic, religious or cultural matters." Moreover, the Court has recognized that these rights of expressive association belong to all manner of groups, regardless of the form in which they are organized. In the *NAACP* case itself, the Court did not even note this factor as a potentially pertinent concern. The NAACP was (and is) a corporation. Many other Supreme Court decisions have likewise unquestioningly and unanimously assumed that the implicit First Amendment freedom of association, along with the explicit First Amendment freedom of speech, applies to for-profit corporations—including the media corporations that have been the focus of many such decisions—as well as various other types of organizations, including labor unions, unincorporated associations, partnerships, and foundations.

What is the freedom of non-association?

Just as the explicit freedom of speech has a counterpart in the implicit freedom not to speak, so too the implicit freedom of expressive association has a counterpart in the implicit freedom not to associate in an expressive sense. Therefore, the Supreme Court has upheld the right of parade organizers to exclude would-be paraders who wanted to march behind banners with messages that contravened the parade organizers' beliefs. In its unanimous 1995 ruling in *Hurley v. Irish-American Gay, Lesbian, and Bisexual Group of Boston* (GLIB), the Supreme Court overturned lower court rulings that enforced the Massachusetts public accommodations law against the South Boston Allied War Veterans Council, "an . . . association of individuals" that organized a "St. Patrick's Day-Evacuation Day" parade. Public accommodations laws, which derive from deep-rooted common law doctrine, require certain private facilities that generally hold themselves open to the public not to discriminate against particular individuals or groups. *Hurley* held that the First Amendment protected the Council from being required to include a GLIB contingent in its parade, notwithstanding the Massachusetts public accommodation law. The Court explained:

> [A] contingent marching behind [GLIB]'s banner would at least bear witness to the fact that some Irish are gay, lesbian, or bisexual, and . . . would suggest their view that people of their sexual orientations have as much claim to unqualified social acceptance as heterosexuals. . . . The parade's organizers may not believe these facts about Irish sexuality to be so, or they may object to unqualified social acceptance of gays and lesbians or have some other reason for wishing to keep GLIB's message out of the parade. But whatever the reason, it boils down to the choice of a speaker not to propound a particular point

of view, and that choice is . . . beyond the government's power to control.

The *Hurley* Court stressed that its holding was viewpoint-neutral, neither endorsing nor disapproving either the Council's message or GLIB's: "Our holding today rests not on any particular view about [either] message. . . . Disapproval of a private speaker's statement does not legitimize use of the [government]'s power to compel the speaker to alter the message by including one more acceptable to others." These very same viewpoint-neutral principles concerning freedom of non-association would also protect the right of "Pride" parade organizers to exclude contingents of marchers with messages they found incompatible with theirs—for example, a contingent marching behind the banner of the South Boston Allied War Veterans Council.

How do we distinguish protected freedom of non-association from impermissible discrimination?

The *Hurley* passage quoted above specifically upheld the parade organizers' implied First Amendment right to "keep GLIB's message out of the parade," not to keep individual GLIB members out of the parade—much less to exclude any individual LGBTQ+ people. If any such individuals, including GLIB members, marched without any signs at all, or marched with signs that the parade organizers deemed compatible with their message, such participation would not have undermined the organizers' freedom of expressive association. Therefore, the organizers would have no First Amendment claim of expressive non-association. In a nutshell, the First Amendment protects speakers' right to dissociate from certain people because of what those people say, but not because of who they are. Correspondingly, public accommodations laws, as well as other sources of law, bar discriminatory treatment of individuals, consistent with fundamental equality norms.

In some cases, groups have asserted that the mere inclusion of certain individuals would necessarily undermine the group message. These cases require detailed fact-specific assessments of the competing expressive and equality concerns in each situation, and Supreme Court Justices (and other judges) have reached differing conclusions, based on their differing factual assessments in particular cases. By a 5–4 vote, the Court held in 2000 that the Boy Scouts of America (BSA) had a First Amendment right to bar a gay man, James Dale, from serving as a scout leader, notwithstanding that this bar violated a state public accommodations law. In contrast, in three cases in the 1980s, the Court held without dissent that several historically all-male organizations (including the Jaycees and the Rotary Club) did not have a First Amendment right to bar women from joining their organizations, as state public accommodations laws required.[7]

Even if a government measure invades First Amendment rights—in these situations by undermining an association's message—that measure would still be constitutional if it survived strict scrutiny: if the government could show that the measure was necessary to promote an important public purpose. In the all-male organization cases, the Court held that any infringement on the organizations' First Amendment expressive association rights that might result from the inclusion of women was necessary to promote the important goal of gender equality. In contrast, in the Boy Scouts case, the Court's narrow majority accepted the BSA's assertions that it "does not want to promote homosexual conduct as a legitimate form of behavior," and that "Dale's presence as an assistant scoutmaster would significantly . . . interfere with the Scouts' choice not to propound a point of view contrary to its beliefs." Furthermore, the majority concluded that the countervailing equality concerns did "not justify such a severe intrusion on the Boy Scouts' rights to freedom of expressive association." In his constitutional law treatise, Berkeley Law School Dean Erwin Chemerinsky provided the following hypothetical examples of a group's "right to discriminate where discrimination is integral to expressive activity": "the Klan likely could exclude African Americans or the Nazi party could exclude Jews because discrimination is a key aspect of their message."

Readers will recognize that this same tension between antidiscrimination laws and First Amendment rights is presented in many recent and ongoing cases about whether photographers, web designers, and other individuals who provide expressive services to the general public must provide these services for same-sex weddings, even if the expressive service providers have conscientious objections to such marriages. (At least some of these expressive service providers stress that they do not discriminate based on customers' identities; rather, they even-handedly decline to provide services for same-sex weddings to anyone who seeks such services, regardless of sexual orientation, while providing other services to everyone, also regardless of sexual orientation.[8]) The lower courts have been divided about these issues, which the Supreme Court has not yet squarely addressed (as of May 2023), although it has a pertinent case on its 2022–23 docket.

What is academic freedom?

The Supreme Court has held that the First Amendment implicitly protects the autonomy of academic institutions to make basic decisions about which faculty members to hire and which students to enroll, as well as what subjects will be researched and taught. The Court has stressed that these rights facilitate the academic institutions' special truth-seeking mission, which benefits not only members of the academic communities themselves, but also our larger society. For example, in a much-quoted passage in a 1967 case, the Court stated: "Our Nation is deeply committed to safeguarding academic freedom, which is of transcendent value to all of us, and not merely to the teachers concerned. That freedom is therefore a special concern of the First Amendment, which does not tolerate laws that cast a pall of orthodoxy over the classroom."

The Court has invoked these academic freedom concerns in cases that struck down McCarthy-era programs targeting faculty members who were suspected of being "subversive," including a state legislative investigation into lectures delivered at a state university and a state "loyalty oath" requirement that each faculty member declare that "I am not and have never been a member of the Communist Party."

More recently, the Court has cited academic freedom concerns as weighing in favor of universities' race-based affirmative action programs for student admissions. In rejecting arguments that such programs violated the Equal Protection Clause, Justice Lewis Powell's influential 1978 opinion in *University of California v. Bakke* invoked the countervailing academic freedom concerns, which a 2003 majority opinion endorsed: "Academic freedom, though not a specifically enumerated constitutional right, long has been . . . a special concern of the First Amendment. The freedom of a university to make its own judgments as to education includes the selection of its student body." Deferring to the universities' judgment that their affirmative action programs would promote student body "diversity," with attendant educational benefits, Powell concluded that "[u]niversities must be accorded the right to select those students who will contribute the most to the robust exchange of ideas."[9]

Who has free speech rights?

Consistent with the Free Speech Clause's open-textured language, which generally bars any government measures abridging the freedom of speech, the Supreme Court has held that this language shields all individuals, as well as groups of individuals. For instance, in accord with the implicit freedom of association, the Court has held that this clause protects groups of people who form various types of organizations—including

unincorporated associations, partnerships, and corporations—
when the organizations engage in expression. The Court has
stressed that organizations facilitate controversial expression
because individuals might well be deterred from engaging in
such expression on their own.

In its 2010 *Citizens United v. FEC* decision, the Court
elucidated why speaker-based speech restrictions, which selectively restrict speech due to the speaker's identity, are as
constitutionally suspect as content-based restrictions, which
selectively restrict speech due to its message. *Citizens United*
involved restrictions on expression by unions, nonprofit
corporations, and for-profit corporations, but the general principles it enforced also apply to other speaker-based restrictions.
For example, immigrants' rights advocates have relied on this
aspect of *Citizens United* to oppose the federal government's
arguments that unauthorized immigrants have no free speech
rights. *Citizens United* explained that content-based and
speaker-based restrictions, "[a]s instruments to censor, . . . are
interrelated: Speech restrictions based on the identity of the
speaker are all too often simply a means to control content."
For instance, unauthorized immigrants have been forceful
advocates of proposed immigration policy reforms, including
the DREAM Act;[10] government threats to punish these particular speakers for this advocacy, including through deportation,
would disproportionately suppress these particular messages.

Even beyond its concern that speaker-based speech
restrictions will suppress certain messages, *Citizens United*
concluded that such restrictions pose additional constitutional
problems; they are inconsistent with the equal rights regarding
expression and democratic participation to which all members
of our society are entitled, regardless of who they are (and also
regardless of what they believe). Finally, the Court pointed out,
by depriving certain parties of the First Amendment right to
speak, government thereby also deprives everyone else of the
First Amendment right to listen to those would-be speakers:

By taking the right to speak from some and giving it to others, the Government deprives the disadvantaged person or class of the right to use speech to strive to establish worth, standing, and respect for the speaker's voice. The Government may not by these means deprive the public of the right and privilege to determine for itself what speech and speakers are worthy of consideration.

Why may the government impose special restrictions on speech by people in public institutions, such as schools?

The First Amendment analysis is appropriately different when government is acting not as a general regulator of the public sphere, enforcing generally applicable laws, but rather as the operator of specific public institutions, with specific public-serving missions. In order to facilitate the government's—and the broader public's—interest in promoting those institutions' missions, government may restrict the speech of people in such institutional contexts more than in the general public sphere. For example, while government employees are at work, they do not have the same free speech rights they have on their own time in a public park: to discuss any issues, to advocate any perspectives, and to use any language they might choose. In short, these institution-based restrictions are permitted not because of who the speakers are in a general sense, but rather because of the specific role they play in the context of a specific government institution. The *Citizens United* decision spelled this out: "The Court has upheld a narrow class of speech restrictions that operate to the disadvantage of certain persons," such as government employees, "but these rulings were based on an interest in allowing governmental entities to perform their functions," not on an interest in suppressing speech by those persons.

Do for-profit corporations have free speech rights?

Many of the Court's most important free speech cases have involved for-profit media corporations, such as the *New York Times*, as well as nonprofit corporations with ideologically diverse agendas—including, for example, the NAACP, which previous answers have already mentioned, as well as both Planned Parenthood and the National Right to Life Committee. Moreover, the Court consistently has recognized that the implied freedom of association protects groups regardless of the form in which they are organized—having first recognized that important right in a case involving a corporation, the NAACP. To be sure, the NAACP was—and is—a nonprofit corporation, but the Court did not even advert to this fact, let alone suggest that it was legally relevant. Therefore, in the controversial 2010 *Citizens United* case, which held that certain limits on corporations' and unions' expenditures for political messages violated these groups' First Amendment rights, it is noteworthy that all nine Justices agreed that corporations (both for-profit and not-for-profit) do have First Amendment rights. The Justices' 5–4 division concerned other issues—in particular, whether there were sufficient justifications for the specific restrictions on corporate and union expression at issue in the case.

This unanimity among the Justices in recognizing the importance of corporate free speech rights sets them apart from the general public and politicians, among whom there is widespread mockery of the proposition that "corporations are people"—to quote critics' common derisive phrase that purports to paraphrase the Court's holdings on point. When viewed in their larger historical and principled context, the Court's many rulings upholding corporate free speech rights are integral to the Court's steadfast protection of individuals' rights to express their views through various types of associations, which is especially important when the views are controversial. From this perspective, it is understandable why both liberal and conservative Justices consistently have endorsed corporate free expression rights (while, again, differing about the constitutionality of particular restrictions on such expression).

Just as a group's corporate form never has been a basis for reducing its freedom of speech or association, the same is true for speech concerning business or economic interests. The Court's very first decision enforcing the implicit freedom of association (in 1958) said that "[o]f course, it is immaterial" what "the beliefs sought to be advanced by association pertain to," including "economic . . . matters." Furthermore, as long ago as 1945, the Court spurned the argument "that the First Amendment's safeguards are wholly inapplicable to business or economic activity." It repudiated the state's position that First Amendment protections should not extend to "an organization" that "is engaged in business activities." The particular organization in that case was a labor union, but the same considerations apply to other organizations also engaged in business activities, including for-profit corporations.

Do minors have free speech rights?

In the 1976 *Planned Parenthood v. Danforth* decision, which upheld minors' constitutional right to abortion under the then-governing precedent of *Roe v. Wade*, the Supreme Court reaffirmed that minors are entitled to all constitutional rights, specifically citing earlier decisions that had upheld minors' free speech rights (as well as other rights). The Court declared: "Constitutional rights do not mature and come into being magically only when one attains the state-defined age of majority. Minors, as well as adults, are protected by the Constitution." Nonetheless, the *Danforth* opinion also observed that "the State has somewhat broader authority to regulate the activities of children than of adults." In support of that statement, the Court cited only one, narrowly focused case concerning minors' general free speech rights (i.e., outside of the public school context), in which it had held those rights to be less extensive than adults': the 1968 *Ginsberg v. New York* decision, ruling that government had more power to bar the distribution of certain sexual expression to minors than to adults.

In contrast with its *Ginsberg* holding, the Court consistently has rejected government arguments that minors should be barred from access to other (i.e., nonsexual) materials "that a legislative body thinks unsuitable for them," including violent materials. In a 2011 decision, the Court said that *Ginsberg* did not vest the government with "a free-floating power to restrict the ideas to which children may be exposed." The Supreme Court has accorded speech with sexual content less First Amendment protection than speech with other content. Therefore, it is not surprising that the Court likewise has accorded minors fewer First Amendment rights concerning expression with sexual content only, but not any other content.

To be sure, the Court has upheld government's special power to regulate certain speech by minors specifically in the public school context. However, those decisions reflect the fact that the government is acting in its special role as the operator of a specific institution—the public schools—and not in its general regulatory capacity. For that reason, the government has more power to restrict the free speech (and other) rights of all members of the public school community, including students and faculty members.

Consistent with the Court's approach of treating minors' general free speech rights (i.e., beyond the public school context) on a par with adults', some of the Court's most important free speech cases, which secure significant free speech rights for everyone, happened to involve plaintiffs who were minors. Indeed, in some of these cases, the minor plaintiffs were school students. That is true, for instance, of the landmark 1943 flag salute case, which eloquently endorsed two major implied First Amendment rights for everyone: freedom of conscience and freedom from government-compelled expression.

Do non-U.S. citizens who are in the United States have free speech rights?

Although the Supreme Court's case law on this issue leaves a major unanswered question, it supports one important major conclusion: Non-citizens who are lawfully present in the United States in any capacity (as either temporary visitors or permanent residents) have the same First Amendment rights as U.S. citizens, with one narrow exception. Before addressing that narrow exception, it is worth underscoring the general rule. As long ago as 1945, substantially before the modern Court began to strongly enforce free speech rights in general, the Court conclusorily stated: "Freedom of speech and of press is accorded aliens residing in this country." The Court treated this as a sufficiently self-evident proposition that it didn't include any explanation. Indeed, that decision cited an even earlier one in which the Court had upheld the free speech rights of a non-citizen resident without even noting his citizenship status, thus indicating its irrelevance to the First Amendment analysis. The Free Speech Clause's text supports that conclusion, since it is framed as a limit on government power generally, not a grant of rights to particular people (again, it provides that "Congress shall make no law . . . abridging the freedom of speech").

Now I will address the sole narrow exception to the general rule that non-citizen lawful residents enjoy full First Amendment rights. In 2012, the Supreme Court affirmed a lower-court decision, *Bluman v. FEC*, upholding a federal statute that barred non-citizens who were temporary U.S. residents from making financial contributions or expenditures in connection with U.S. elections. The Court long has held that any such campaign finance restrictions limit the political expression that is especially important in our representative democracy, and hence these restrictions are subject to intense judicial review. That said, precisely because non-citizens who are temporarily in the United States are not members of our political community, restrictions on their expressive activities that are "intimately related to the process of democratic self-government" have been held to satisfy even demanding judicial review. The *Bluman* decision ruled that the restrictions at issue were necessary for promoting the important interest in "preventing foreign influence over the U.S. political process." The decision stressed, though, that its holding was confined to the particular facts at issue in that case, and that this holding might not extend to similar but distinct factual situations. For example, the decision posited that the challenged restriction might violate the First Amendment rights of "lawful permanent residents who have a more significant attachment to the United States than the temporary resident plaintiffs in this case."

The major unresolved issue concerning resident non-citizens' First Amendment rights, which the Supreme Court has not explicitly addressed, is whether such rights extend to the estimated 11.4 million non-citizen residents who are in the United States unlawfully. The Court's decisions to date, including the 1945 case quoted above, have included broad, unqualified statements recognizing the First Amendment rights of resident non-citizens. These former cases, however, involved non-citizens who were lawfully residing in the United States. Therefore, it is not clear whether the Court would extend the same holding to non-citizens residing in the United States unlawfully.

This issue was squarely presented in a class action lawsuit filed in 2015 by Central American mothers who were seeking asylum in the United States for themselves and their children, and were imprisoned in detention facilities while their asylum cases were pending. Protesting this detention, the mothers went on hunger strike; they alleged that the government punished their hunger strike in several ways, including by threatening to take away their children. The lawsuit contended that, since the hunger strike constituted expressive conduct, the alleged punishment violated the First Amendment. In opposing the lawsuit, the U.S. Department of Justice argued that, even assuming plaintiffs' First Amendment claims would be valid if raised by a citizen or lawful resident, such claims were not valid by virtue of the plaintiffs' non-lawful presence in the United States. In response, immigrants' rights advocates stressed the condemnation of speaker-based speech restrictions that the Court's 2010 *Citizens United* decision set out. For instance, law professor Michael Kagan wrote: "*Citizens United* . . . articulates a compelling, progressive reason to encourage a diversity of voices in public life, and to closely scrutinize any government attempt to exclude a speaker based on who they are." The Central American mother plaintiffs voluntarily dismissed their lawsuit, so this key issue was not resolved even by the trial court in that case, and the U.S. Supreme Court still has not addressed it.

4

SPEECH RESTRICTIONS THAT THE FIRST AMENDMENT PERMITS

What kinds of connections are required between speech and harm to justify speech restrictions?

> The real issue in every free speech controversy is this: whether the state can punish all words which have some tendency, however remote, to bring about acts in violation of law, or only words which directly incite to acts in violation of law.
>
> Harvard Law School professor Zechariah Chafee,
>
> 1920

There have been serious debates about the First Amendment questions that this book has already addressed, such as what expression constitutes "speech" within the Amendment's ambit, and which individuals and groups should have speech rights. The most important ongoing debates, however, continue to focus on the most challenging questions about distinguishing between protected and punishable speech under any legal system (or from a philosophical perspective), which Professor Chafee flagged in the above epigraph: What kinds of connections must there be between the speech and potential harms to which it might contribute, in order to justify restrictions on that speech? And, relatedly, to which kinds of potential harms must the speech contribute? Should certain harms resulting from speech not justify restrictions?

All of us have experienced many kinds of speech-induced harms that, by common consensus, should not warrant restricting the speech. These harms range from wounded pride caused by a supervisor's criticism of our work performance, to a broken heart caused by a former romantic partner's break-up message, to anxiety caused by a government official's warning about an impending natural disaster in our immediate geographical area. What are the appropriate distinctions between these kinds of speech-induced harms, which do not warrant speech restrictions, and other speech-induced harms, which do?[1] And for the latter harms, beyond the type of connection that must be shown between the speech and the harm, what other prerequisites should there be to legitimize speech restrictions? For example, should it matter what the speaker's intent was?

These challenging questions have fueled philosophical debates about free speech from time immemorial, and have also resulted in varying legal rules, including those embodied in current First Amendment law. Before summarizing the pertinent legal rules, this book first addresses the most important general considerations that the Supreme Court has considered in crafting them—in other words, the major questions, and the Court's answers, that provide the general First Amendment framework. Although the questions have profound philosophical implications, the Court's answers also resonate with common sense.

What is the most dangerous speech, which the First Amendment lets government outlaw?

Supreme Court Justices and others who champion strong free speech protection are acutely aware of speech's dangerous potential. Indeed, such individuals support robust freedom of speech precisely because they appreciate speech's great power—a power to do much harm, as well as much good. The Supreme Court made this point, for instance, in a 2011 decision that reaffirmed our national commitment "to protect even hurtful speech on public issues to ensure that we do not stifle public debate."

Recognizing the dangers of both speech and censorship, the Court has formulated rules to outlaw the instances of both that are the most dangerous. The speech that is the most dangerous has a tight and direct causal and temporal connection to certain serious harms, and these harms must go beyond disapproval of the speech's message. Thus, speech may not be restricted solely based on any harm attributed to its message—or "content"—considered alone. In contrast, speech may be restricted based on a specific harm that directly results from its message being conveyed in certain circumstances—that is, in "context." To be restricted, the speech must either immediately cause the pertinent harm or threaten to do so imminently. A classic example of speech in the first category is expression that violates someone's intellectual property rights because it is sufficiently identical to a copyrighted work. A classic example of speech in the second category is intentional incitement of imminent illegal or violent conduct that is likely to happen imminently.

The "emergency" principle is a shorthand label for government's power to restrict speech that immediately causes or imminently threatens specific serious harms.[2] This term captures the key rationale for permitting speech restrictions in these situations: that there is no feasible alternative strategy to avert the harm. Short of such an emergency, however, government should use other harm-averting measures. An often-quoted explanation of this key concept comes from the 1927 opinion by Supreme Court Justice Brandeis in *Whitney v. California*. At that time, decades before the Court began to adopt its modern speech-protective principles, it allowed government to restrict speech that had only a loose, indirect, speculative connection to potential harm. Accordingly, the *Whitney* Court approved the criminal punishment of expression advocating socialism on the ground that it might induce audience members to engage in illegal or violent conduct. In contrast,

Brandeis's separate opinion (which Justice Holmes also joined) presciently advocated the much stricter "intentional incitement" standard that the modern Court unanimously adopted in 1969; Brandeis's opinion also articulated the emergency principle:

> [E]ven advocacy of [lawbreaking] . . . is not a justification for denying free speech where the advocacy falls short of incitement and there is nothing to indicate that [it] would be immediately acted on. . . . [N]o danger flowing from speech can be deemed [punishable], unless the incidence of the evil apprehended is so imminent that it may befall before there is opportunity for full discussion. . . . Only an emergency can justify repression.

What is the most dangerous censorship, which the First Amendment outlaws?

The most dangerous censorship constitutes the counterpart of the most dangerous speech. The closer the connection between speech and a serious harm, the more dangerous the speech. Correspondingly, the more remote the connection between speech and a serious harm, the more dangerous the censorship. When government officials are allowed to restrict speech on the rationale that it might indirectly cause or contribute to potential harm at some future point, they can invoke this speculative harm as a pretext for censoring their political opponents or critics—precisely the censorship that is most dangerous in our representative democracy. Recall Justice Holmes's warning that "[e]very idea is an incitement."

Suppressing speech based on its feared attenuated connection to future harm not only undermines the individual liberty of each member of "We the People" to choose what expression to convey and to receive; it also undermines our collective sovereignty, by stifling the vigorous debate and dissent that has been saluted as "the lifeblood of democracy." This is why the harms that warrant speech restrictions consistent with the emergency principle are serious harms that are independent of the disfavored nature of the speech's message. This central precept, which is generally described as "content neutrality" or "viewpoint neutrality," bars government from restricting speech solely due to its disfavored content—that is, its message, ideas, or viewpoint. The Supreme Court has warned that a content-based speech restriction permits officials to "manipulate public debate" by "[suppressing] unpopular ideas or information." In contrast, when government restricts speech because, considered in context, the speech inflicts an independent harm—such as violating intellectual property rights or intentionally inciting imminent violence—"there is no realistic possibility that" the government is engaging in "official suppression of ideas."

What are "prophylactic rules," which err in favor of protecting too much speech, rather than too little?

A common explanation for the presumption of innocence, as well as other rights of accused people in our criminal legal system, is that "it is better for ten guilty people to go free, than for one innocent person to be convicted." In other words, acknowledging that no rule can infallibly separate the guilty from the innocent, these "prophylactic" or preventative rules are deliberately designed to over-protect criminal defendants' rights, as preferable to the alternative of under-protecting them. Likewise, concerning our fundamental First Amendment free speech rights, the Supreme Court has laid out some prophylactic rules, which intentionally shield some expression that would be constitutionally punishable, as the appropriate price for avoiding the punishment and deterrence of speech that should be constitutionally protected. As the Court recognizes, unless speech-restricting doctrines are narrowly crafted, people will understandably engage in excessive self-censorship, refraining from even constitutionally protected expression that enforcing authorities might nonetheless deem to be unprotected and therefore seek to punish.

A famous case in which the Court articulated these general considerations is its unanimous 1964 ruling in *New York Times v. Sullivan*. In order to prevent excessive self-censorship in criticizing public officials, for fear that the officials could pursue credible (even if ultimately unsuccessful) defamation lawsuits against their critics, the Court held that the First Amendment required additional limits on such lawsuits, beyond those imposed by traditional defamation tort law. Concerning the false statements at issue, the Court ruled, defamation plaintiffs who were public officials had to show that the defendant either knew the statements were false or uttered them with reckless disregard as to their truth or falsity. Moreover, public official defamation plaintiffs had to make this showing under the more demanding "clear and convincing evidence" standard, in contrast with the usual civil litigation standard of "preponderance of the evidence."

In short, the Court deliberately adopted a rule that would result in First Amendment protection for not only some lies, but even some lies that damaged some public officials' reputations. The Court's explanation for this counterintuitive result sheds light on other prophylactic First Amendment rules that also intentionally immunize certain harmful speech that would be constitutionally punishable. Therefore, it is worth quoting this rationale at some length.

> [W]e consider this case against the background of a profound national commitment to the principle that debate on public issues should be uninhibited, robust, and wide-open, and that it may well include vehement, caustic, and sometimes unpleasantly sharp attacks on government and public officials. . . . The constitutional protection does not turn upon the truth, popularity, or social utility of the ideas and beliefs which are offered. . . .

[E]rroneous statement is inevitable in free debate, and . . . it must be protected if the freedoms of expression are to have the breathing space that they need . . . to survive. . . .

Injury to official reputation affords no more warrant for repressing speech . . . than does factual error. . . . Criticism of . . . official conduct does not lose its constitutional protection merely because it is effective criticism, and hence diminishes . . . official reputations. . . .

[W]ould-be critics of official conduct may be deterred from voicing their criticism, even though it is believed to be true and even though it is, in fact, true, because of doubt whether it can be proved in court or fear of the expense of having to do so. They tend to make only statements which steer far wider of the unlawful zone . . . thus [dampening] . . . public debate.

Sullivan's prophylactic approach, protecting even some speech that causes some harm, reflects a judgment that pervades contemporary First Amendment law: The harms of "excessive" free speech, while real, are less problematic than the harms of excessive government censorship and self-censorship.

What factors affect whether the First Amendment permits particular speech restrictions?

Prior answers have noted the case-specific, fact-intensive nature of the Supreme Court rulings that constitute First Amendment free speech law, turning on the details concerning not only the targeted speech—in terms of both content and context—but also the particular restriction at issue. In addition, the factors that the Court considers, and its analytical approach, vary from case to case. The prominent constitutional scholar Erwin Chemerinsky has flagged this challenging aspect of this body of law: "Part of what makes First Amendment analysis difficult is that . . . there is no prescribed order for analysis. . . . [I]t is not possible to comprehensively flowchart the First Amendment as a defined series of questions in a required sequential order." That said, in many cases, the Court has repeatedly cited certain factual considerations that affect its First Amendment free speech analysis.

How fact-specific is First Amendment law?

The Free Speech Clause unqualifiedly bars any law "abridging the freedom of speech," without drawing explicit distinctions among various instances of "speech" depending on either their content or their context. Yet, in answering the challenging specific questions it has confronted about whether to deem any particular speech restriction an impermissible "abridgement" of "the freedom of speech," the Court has considered both the content and context of the speech.

Given the intensely fact-specific nature of the Court's analysis, a change in one contextual factor could result in a different bottom-line outcome. Let me cite one recent illustration, arising from a 2016 campaign rally for then-presidential-candidate Donald Trump. Referring to some anti-Trump demonstrators, the candidate urged his supporters to "get 'em out of here." Some demonstrators claimed that, in the wake of Trump's statements, some Trump supporters removed them from the rally, punching and shoving them in the process. Reviewing the many pertinent facts that bore on the key question of whether Trump could be held culpable for "intentionally inciting" his supporters' assaultive conduct, the federal appellate court concluded that one phrase in Trump's exhortation to his supporters required a negative answer to that question: "Don't hurt 'em."

Likewise, whether Trump's speech to his supporters on January 6, 2021 amounted to punishable intentional incitement turns on the many factual details that illuminate whether his remarks satisfied that fact-based standard. One statement in Trump's January 6 speech is similar to his just-quoted 2016 statement, which the appellate court had deemed exculpatory in that case. On January 6, Trump said: "I know that everyone here will soon be marching over to the Capitol building to peacefully and patriotically make your voices heard." In contrast, those who urge that Trump's January 6 speech did constitute punishable intentional incitement stress these other statements he also made, and the explosive context in which he made them: "We fight like hell. And if you don't fight like hell, you're not going to have a country anymore."

In its hundreds of free speech rulings over the past century, the Supreme Court recurrently has stressed five major categories of factual considerations as significantly affecting its analysis:

1. Content/topic—What is said?
2. Communications medium—How is it said?
3. Place—Where is it said?
4. Speaker—Who says it?
5. Type of regulation.

The next set of questions addresses how each of these factors has affected the Court's free speech analysis.

How is First Amendment analysis affected by the content or topic of the speech?

Does the First Amendment protect only speech that contains information or ideas?

Even the pre-modern Supreme Court rejected arguments that First Amendment protection should be limited only to speech that contains particular content—namely, information or ideas. In a significant 1948 decision, *Winters v. New York*, the Court overturned a ruling by New York State's highest court, which had held that the First Amendment did not shield publications that "so massed their collection of pictures and stories of bloodshed and of lust as to become vehicles for inciting violent and depraved crimes against the person." The New York court had upheld a bookseller's criminal conviction for selling various magazines and comic books, including *True Detective*. Reversing this holding, the Supreme Court rejected the argument that the First Amendment applied only to "information" or "ideas," explaining: "The line between the informing and the entertaining is too elusive. . . . Everyone is familiar with instances of propaganda through fiction. What is one man's amusement, teaches another's doctrine."

Does the First Amendment protect speech that constitutes only self-expression?

The Court's longstanding recognition that "freedom of speech" is not confined only to expression that communicates information or ideas has the following corollary: Freedom of speech embraces expression that may not communicate anything at all to any third party, but rather constitutes solely individual self-expression. In fact, one of the age-old rationales for speech freedom is that it enables individuals to develop their own sense of identity, and to express their feelings, as well as their thoughts. This was one of many significant points that the Court made in its landmark 1971 *Cohen v. California* decision. Upholding a young man's right to express his strong opposition to the Vietnam War–era draft with the expletive "fuck," which was then considered shockingly taboo, the Court explained:

> [M]uch linguistic expression serves a dual communicative function: it conveys not only ideas capable of relatively precise, detached explication, but otherwise inexpressible emotions as well. In fact, words are often chosen as much for their emotive as their cognitive force. We cannot sanction the view that the Constitution,

while solicitous of the cognitive content of individual speech, has little or no regard for that emotive function which, practically speaking, may often be the more important element of the overall message sought to be communicated.

Does the First Amendment protect only speech that has some "value"?

In a 1946 decision, *Hannegan v. Esquire*, the Court rejected the argument that the publisher of a periodical who applies for the favorable second-class mail rates "must convince the Postmaster General that his publication positively contributes to the public good," explaining:

> Under our system of government, there is an accommodation for the widest varieties of tastes and ideas. . . . [A] requirement that literature or art conform to some norm prescribed by an official smacks of an ideology foreign to our system. From the multitude of competing offerings, the public will pick and choose. What seems to one to be trash may have for others fleeting or even enduring value.

Likewise, in the 1948 *Winters v. New York* decision, the Justices extended First Amendment protection to the publications at issue (magazines and comic books depicting criminal and sexual conduct) even though "we can see nothing of any possible value to society" in them. Nonetheless, the Court concluded, these publications "are as much entitled to . . . protection . . . as the best of literature." While he dissented from the majority's ruling on other grounds, Justice Frankfurter endorsed this particular proposition with language signaling that it was not even subject to debate: "Wholly neutral futilities, *of course*, come under the protection of free speech as fully as do Keats' poems or Donne's sermons" [emphasis added].

The Court has generally continued to reject the argument that speech must have certain value as a prerequisite for First Amendment protection, and the modern Supreme Court has done so with increasingly rare exceptions. Just as the content-neutrality principle preserves individuals' rights to make their own determinations about the value of particular political ideas, it also preserves these same rights regarding "esthetic and moral judgments about art and literature." The Court has proclaimed that all such judgments "are for the individual to make, not for the Government to decree, even with the mandate or approval of a majority."

Notwithstanding the predominant theme in First Amendment decisions that the amendment protects even expression without "any possible value," the Court also has issued some decisions that run counter to this theme. The most important of these counterpoint decisions—which the Court has never expressly overruled, even though many subsequent decisions are inconsistent with it—is *Chaplinsky v. New Hampshire*, decided in 1942. *Chaplinsky's* central passage states:

> There are certain well defined and narrowly limited classes of speech, the prevention and punishment of which have never been thought to raise any Constitutional problem. These include the lewd and obscene, the profane, the libelous, and the insulting or "fighting" words—those which, by their very utterance, inflict injury or tend to incite an immediate breach of the peace.... [S]uch utterances are no essential part of any exposition of ideas, and are of such slight social value as a step to truth that any benefit that may be derived from them is clearly outweighed by the social interest in order and morality.

Readers will observe that the above-described *Winters* decision, issued only 6 years later, squarely repudiated core elements of this *Chaplinsky* passage in striking down New York's ban on publications depicting "bloodshed and lust." *Winters* expressly rejected *Chaplinsky*'s assertion, which the defenders of the New York law understandably had invoked, that the First Amendment "applies only to the exposition of ideas." Moreover, *Winters* rejected *Chaplinsky*'s indication that the First Amendment applies only to expression that has more than "slight social value" and that contributes "to truth."

One explanation for this dichotomy is that the *Chaplinsky* passage was mostly "dicta"— statements in judicial opinions that are not directly relevant to the particular issue in that case (which in *Chaplinsky* was only whether the expression at issue constituted punishable "fighting words"). In contrast with the Court's "holdings"—its actual rationales for its specific resolution of the issues in the case—dicta are not accorded precedential weight precisely because they do not necessarily reflect the same focused analysis as holdings. When the Supreme Court actually had to decide whether government could restrict speech on the rationale that it was "no essential part of any exposition of ideas," and had only "slight social value as a step to truth"—as it had to do in *Winters*—the Court answered those questions with a resounding "No!"

Notwithstanding the Court's departure from *Chaplinsky*'s dicta as long ago as its 1948 *Winters* ruling, it has continued to issue some decisions that incorporate the *Chaplinsky* dicta's central concept: that certain content-defined categories of speech have no value, or only "low value," and therefore that the First Amendment leaves such speech either wholly unprotected or less protected than speech with other content. Consistent with the modern Court's increasingly strong enforcement of the content-neutrality principle, the Court has steadily reduced the number and scope of such content-defined categories of unprotected or less-protected speech that it formerly recognized. For instance, in a 1975 case, declaring that "a State cannot foreclose the exercise of constitutional rights by mere labels," the Court rejected earlier rulings that speech could be denied First Amendment protection solely because it was labeled "commercial" based on the subject it addressed. Furthermore, in a landmark 2010 ruling, the Court announced that it would not add any new content-based categories of unprotected or less-protected speech to the few remaining, "narrowly defined" content-based categories of speech that historically had been excluded from full First Amendment protection.

The only context in which the Supreme Court still enforces an explicit requirement that expression must have some value as a prerequisite for First Amendment protection is the obscenity doctrine. "Obscenity" constitutes a Court-defined category of sexual expression that is excluded from First Amendment protection; one element of the definition is that the material lacks "serious" value. Conversely, if the material is deemed to have such value, it does come within the First Amendment's protective scope.

The Court also has invoked the "lesser value" rationale to relegate several other categories of sexual expression, beyond the obscenity exception, to less First Amendment protection than speech about other topics. In a 1976 decision that upheld content-based zoning restrictions for "adult" movie theaters (i.e., theaters showing sexually explicit films), which would have been unconstitutional as applied to theaters showing movies with other expressive content, Justice John Paul Stevens's majority opinion asserted: "[F]ew of us would march our sons and daughters off to war to preserve the citizen's right to see [the film] 'Specified Sexual Activities' exhibited in the theaters of our choice."

On behalf of the four dissenters, Justice Potter Stewart retorted that this assertion "stands" the core content-neutrality principle "on its head":

For if the guarantees of the First Amendment were reserved for expression that more than a "few of us" would take up arms to defend, then the right of free expression would be defined and circumscribed by current popular opinion. The guarantees of the Bill of Rights were designed to protect against precisely such majoritarian limitations on individual liberty.

Stewart's dissent presciently concluded: "I can only interpret today's decision as an aberration." Indeed, that 1976 decision has become increasingly anomalous, and that is also true for the Court's decisions enforcing the obscenity exception. Instead, modern First Amendment law, including most rulings about sexual expression, honors the predominant value-neutral perspective that traces all the way back to the 1940s *Hannegan* and *Winters* decisions.

How protected is "political" speech?

The Court uses the adjective "political" to designate not only expression that is literally about politics (e.g., a candidate's campaign speeches) but also all expression about matters of public concern. It long has treated all such speech as especially important, given its essential role in our democratic republic. Observing that "[s]peech is an essential mechanism of democracy, for it is the means to hold officials accountable to the people," the Court has concluded that "speech on public issues occupies the highest rung of the hierarchy of First Amendment values, and is entitled to special protection." For this reason, in striking down particular speech restrictions pursuant to its usual fact-specific contextual analysis, a factor that the Court regularly has stressed is that the speech addresses a matter of public concern.

The highly protected category of "political"/"public concern" speech of course includes expression directly regarding political campaigns. As the Supreme Court stated, the First Amendment "has its fullest and most urgent application to speech uttered during a campaign for political office." This is why modern Justices have overwhelmingly concurred that serious First Amendment concerns are raised by campaign finance restrictions, because they limit the amount of money available to disseminate this "most [urgently]" important expression, hence limiting its dissemination. Accordingly, the Justices also have concurred that any such restriction violates the First Amendment unless government can prove that it sufficiently promotes other important values, although they have strongly disagreed about whether the government has satisfied that burden of proof regarding particular restrictions.

The Supreme Court has defined "political"/"public concern" speech broadly, to encompass essentially any topic in which the public and the news media are interested. In many cases regarding various First Amendment doctrines, the Court has emphasized that the expression addressed a matter of public concern as a factor supporting its protection. For example, the Court has issued two decisions about First Amendment limits on tort actions for "intentional infliction of emotional distress," which arose from offensive, hateful speech. In concluding that the First Amendment barred both lawsuits, the Court stressed that the allegedly tortious speech addressed matters of public concern. In contrast, it left open the possibility that the First Amendment might not bar recovery for similar speech that addressed only private matters. Likewise, the Court has extended some protection to government employees' speech about matters of public concern but no protection to their speech about other matters.

Let me cite one more example of the multiple lines of cases in which the public concern content of the speech at issue has tipped the balance in favor of its protection. The Court has stressed this factor in a series of rulings that the First Amendment barred the specific invasion-of-privacy claims at issue, arising from the publication of sensitive information about certain individuals. For instance, in a 2001 decision, the Court overturned judgments against a radio station and its reporter for having broadcast the recording of an illegally intercepted phone conversation between two teachers' union leaders, about contentious ongoing negotiations with the local school board; the plaintiffs had sued under federal and state statutes barring non-consensual wiretapping. In addition to stressing that the media defendants themselves did not participate in the illegal interception, the Court also noted that "[i]n this case, privacy concerns give way when balanced against the interest in publishing matters of public importance."

How protected is sexual speech?

In contrast with speech about matters of public concern, which the Court has treated as especially deserving of First Amendment protection, the Court historically has treated certain speech about sex as especially undeserving of such protection. It has treated two subsets of sexual expression—obscenity and child pornography—as completely excluded from First Amendment protection, and it has treated three additional subsets of sexual expression as entitled to less First Amendment protection than speech with other content.

Although the Court's failure to extend full First Amendment protection to these five subcategories of sexual expression has been controversial, they still constitute only a small portion of all sexual expression. In contrast, most sexual expression has received full First Amendment protection. The Court emphasized this fact even in its 1957 decision that first set out the obscenity exception, explaining:

> The portrayal of sex . . . is not itself sufficient reason to deny material . . . constitutional protection. . . . Sex, a great and mysterious motive force in human life, has indisputably been a subject of absorbing interest to mankind through the ages; it is one of the vital problems of human interest and public concern.

Before summarizing the five subsets of sexual expression that traditionally have been wholly or partially excluded from First Amendment protection, I want to put them in historical context: Most of the pertinent cases are quite old, and they have become increasingly incongruous with the modern Court's increasingly speech-protective trajectory. Moreover, while the Court has not recently reexamined its older decisions relegating certain sexual expression to less-than-full First Amendment protection, its more recent decisions on point consistently have declined to expand the scope of such unprotected and less-protected expression.

What is constitutionally unprotected "obscenity"?

The Court initially articulated the obscenity doctrine in 1957. It applied that label to a subset of sexually explicit speech, defined by its content, and held it to be completely excluded from First Amendment protection. In its 1973 decision in *Paris Adult Theatre v. Slaton*, the Court reexamined this controversial exception to general free speech principles, but reaffirmed it by a 5–4 vote. Since then, many individual Justices (across the ideological spectrum), as well as First Amendment experts, have continued to urge the Court to eliminate the obscenity exception as inconsistent with the First Amendment, but the Court has not yet even reconsidered that exception, let alone repudiating it.

Although the Supreme Court's obscenity exception is controversial, it is narrower in several respects than older concepts of obscenity that had been enforced in Great Britain and the United States. For a work to be considered obscene, it now must be judged as a whole, so that an isolated passage would no longer be enough to condemn it. Furthermore, the work, taken as a whole, must appeal to the "prurient" interest in sex (which the Court has defined as an interest that is "sick and morbid" rather than "normal and healthy"), and the work must be "patently offensive" to "an average person, applying contemporary community standards." This means that the work must be evaluated in light of evolving community norms of tolerance, from an objective perspective; in contrast, older tests judged a work from the perspective of "the most susceptible" community members. Finally, the current test adds a requirement that was absent from older obscenity concepts: The work, taken as a whole, must lack "serious literary, artistic, political, or scientific value," as judged by contemporary national standards; the focus on national standards means that more parochial perspectives about a work's lack of serious value will not suffice to brand it as obscene.

While the current obscenity definition is less overbroad than its forebears, it still poses vagueness problems, failing to provide sufficient guidance to "a person of ordinary intelligence" about what expression is outlawed. Can such a person distinguish, for example, between a "sick" and a "healthy" interest in sex, in determining whether certain expression appeals to the "prurient" interest in sex? And is it fair—and sufficiently speech-protective—to require someone to risk criminal prosecution and even punishment for reaching the "wrong" conclusion about this issue? The best-known Supreme Court statement about the obscenity doctrine powerfully captures its intractable vagueness. Justice Potter Stewart candidly acknowledged that he could "perhaps . . . never succeed in intelligibly" defining obscenity, instead expressly relying on his personal, subjective perceptions: "I know it when I see it."

Paris Adult acknowledged that there is no evidence that obscene expression directly causes or threatens any imminent harm, thus underscoring that the obscenity exception is squarely inconsistent with the emergency principle, as well as the content-neutrality principle. Instead, the majority relied on the loose "bad tendency" standard that the Court had jettisoned in other modern First Amendment contexts. The *Paris Adult* opinion said that obscenity could be criminalized based on "unprovable assumptions" that "commerce in obscene materials" has "a tendency to exert a corrupting and debasing impact leading to antisocial behavior." Obscenity is now the only content-defined category of expression that is constitutionally unprotected solely due to disapproval or generalized, unsubstantiated fear of its message.

The undue vagueness that afflicts the obscenity exception has been critiqued by Justices all across the Court's ideological spectrum. For example, in a 1987 case, three Justices—two liberals and one moderate—indicted "the vagueness inherent in criminal obscenity statutes." In a separate opinion, the Court's leading arch-conservative at the time, Antonin Scalia, echoed that judgment, complaining that "at least" the serious value prong of the obscenity definition is marred by the "lack of an ascertainable standard," thus indicating that either or both of the other two prongs (requiring that the work must be "patently offensive" and appeal to the "prurient interest" in sex) might also share this fundamental flaw. Observing that the "serious value" criterion cannot be subject to "an objective assessment" because it essentially reflects matters of "taste," Scalia concluded: "Just as there is no use arguing about taste, there is no use litigating about it."

Although the Court has not accepted invitations to overturn the obscenity exception, it also has declined two kinds of invitations to expand that exception. First, the Court's "unprovable assumptions" about obscenity's assertedly negative impacts specifically focused on, "commerce in obscene" materials. Accordingly, even Justices who supported criminalizing the public distribution or display of obscene materials voted to strike down a law criminalizing the mere possession of such materials. In its unanimous 1969 ruling on point, the Court declared: "If the First Amendment means anything, it means that a State has no business telling a man, sitting alone in his own house, what books he may read or what films he may watch. Our whole constitutional heritage rebels at the thought of giving government the power to control men's minds." In that case, the government had surmised that "exposure to obscene material may lead to deviant sexual behavior or crimes of sexual violence." Consistent with its general repudiation of the former "bad tendency" approach, the Court rejoined that "[t]he State may no more prohibit mere possession of obscene matter on the ground that it may lead to antisocial conduct than it may prohibit possession of chemistry books on the ground that they may lead to the manufacture of homemade spirits." Or, one might add, the manufacture of homemade bombs.

The Court also has repeatedly rejected government invitations to expand the obscenity exception in a second significant respect: It consistently has refused to extend that exception to expression with nonsexual content. For example, in 1971 the Court dismissed the contention that wearing a jacket with the slogan "Fuck the Draft" in a courthouse could be punished as obscenity, explaining that constitutionally unprotected obscenity "must be, in some significant way, erotic." Likewise, the Court has consistently rejected government efforts to outlaw expression with violent or other controversial but nonsexual content under laws that track the Court's 1973 definition of constitutionally unprotected obscenity. As the Court declared in one such case, in 2010: "[T]he obscenity exception . . . does not cover whatever a legislature finds shocking, but only depictions of sexual conduct."

What is constitutionally unprotected "obscenity as to minors"?

In the 1968 *Ginsberg v. New York* decision, the Supreme Court upheld an obscenity conviction of a bookseller who had sold "girlie magazines" to a 16-year-old, even though the Court acknowledged that the magazines would not constitute obscenity in any other context. The New York statute that *Ginsberg* upheld tailored its general obscenity definition by inserting the qualification "as to minors" for each element of the definition.[3] For example, one element of the general obscenity concept is that the work, taken as a whole, must lack serious value. Yet, under the New York statute, even if the material was found to have serious value for adults, it could still be found to lack such value "as to minors."

Just as the Court has declined to extend the general obscenity exception to violent material, it also has declined to extend the obscenity-as-to-minors concept to violent material. In 2011, the Court struck down a California statute—similar to other state statutes—that outlawed the sale of certain violent video games to minors, with statutory language that tracked the obscenity-as-to-minors concept. Again stressing that the obscenity doctrine applies only to sexual materials, the Court distinguished *Ginsberg* and concluded that because "California [may] not . . . prohibit selling offensively violent works *to adults*" [emphasis in original], it may not do so regarding minors either.

Further limiting *Ginsberg*'s reach in the internet context, the Court has struck down federal statutes that outlawed "indecent" and "patently offensive" online expression on a child-protection rationale. In contrast with the minor-specific ban on magazine sales that the Court upheld in *Ginsberg*, which did not prevent any magazine sales to adults, the Court has emphasized that online communications cannot be suppressed as to minors without also suppressing them as to adults, given the internet's design. Even assuming for the sake of argument (but not concluding) that the government has a sufficiently compelling interest in shielding minors from such expression, the Court reasoned, measures that also deprive adults of access to it are not necessary/the least restrictive alternative for protecting children; the children's interests could be protected by user-end blocking and filtering software that would not constrict adults' free speech rights.

Is the Supreme Court likely to create new content-defined categories of unprotected speech, similar to the obscenity exception?

The Court-created obscenity doctrine (created in 1957, reaffirmed in 1973, and not reexamined since then) is an outlier in contemporary First Amendment law. When the pre-modern

Court first defined the subset of sexual expression that it labeled "obscenity" and held to be excluded from the First Amendment, it had not yet embraced the content-neutrality or emergency principles that it now consistently enforces. Instead the Court adhered to the 1942 *Chaplinsky* decision, which had broadly supported government power to restrict speech it deemed to be "no essential part of any exposition of ideas, and . . . of such slight social value as a step to truth that any benefit . . . from [such speech] is clearly outweighed by the social interest in order and morality."

In a landmark 2010 decision (by an 8-1 vote), the Court completely repudiated that speech-suppressive rationale of the *Chaplinsky* case. Paraphrasing the just-quoted statement from *Chaplinsky*, the government had asked the Court to treat certain depictions of animal cruelty as beyond the First Amendment pale, arguing that "[w]hether a given category of speech enjoys First Amendment protection depends upon a categorical balancing of the value of the speech against its societal costs." The Court decisively rejected that argument, in unusually strong language:

> As a free-floating test for First Amendment coverage, that sentence is startling and dangerous. The First Amendment's guarantee of free speech does not extend only to categories of speech that survive an ad hoc balancing of relative social costs and benefits. The First Amendment itself reflects a judgment by the American people that the benefits of its restrictions on the Government outweigh the costs. Our Constitution forecloses any attempt to revise that judgment simply on the basis that some speech is not worth it.

Consistent with this general premise, the Court announced that it would not add any new content-based categories of unprotected or less-protected speech to the few remaining, "narrowly defined" content-based categories of speech that historically had been excluded from full First Amendment protection.[4]

What is constitutionally unprotected child pornography?

Because obscenity is constitutionally unprotected solely due to its disapproved message, it is distinguishable in a critical respect from the only other subset of sexual speech that is also constitutionally unprotected: child pornography. The Court has strictly confined the concept of constitutionally unprotected child pornography to sexually explicit depictions of actual minors. Because minors are legally incapable of consenting to pose for sexually explicit photos or films, by definition any such material results from—and constitutes a record of—the minors' abuse and exploitation. The Court has stressed that the justification for outlawing child pornography is to protect children from the inevitable harm they endure from the production process, and not solely disapproval of the material's content, considered apart from the production process. Thus, in sharp contrast with the Court's rationale for excluding obscenity from First Amendment protection, it rationalized its relatively narrow concept of constitutionally unprotected child pornography as satisfying both the emergency and content-neutrality principles.[5]

This fundamental distinction between the rationales for the obscenity and child pornography exclusions from First Amendment protection was underscored by the Court's 2002 decision in *Ashcroft v. Free Speech Coalition*. That case struck down a federal statute that outlawed "virtual child pornography": sexually explicit depictions that "appeared" to depict minors, but were made without using actual minors, instead using youthful-looking adults or computer morphing techniques. The Court highlighted the content-neutral nature of its prior holding that government may outlaw "real child pornography" because that "was based upon how it was made, not on what it communicated."

Free Speech Coalition also rejected the government's further argument for outlawing virtual child pornography: that it "whets the appetites of pedophiles and encourages them to engage in illegal conduct." The Court castigated this attempted resurrection of the discredited bad tendency test, while strongly reaffirming the emergency principle in general and the pertinent concept of punishable incitement in particular: "The mere tendency of speech to encourage unlawful acts is not a sufficient reason for banning it. . . . First Amendment freedoms are most in danger when the government seeks to control thought. . . . The government may not prohibit speech because it increases the chance an unlawful act will be committed at some indefinite future time."

What are the additional subsets of sexual expression that the Court has held to be entitled only to less First Amendment protection than speech about other topics?

In addition to obscenity and child pornography, which are completely excluded from First Amendment protection, the Court also has treated three other categories of sexual speech as entitled to less First Amendment protection than speech with other content. In contrast with obscenity, which is singled out solely due to its disapproved content, and hence is defined wholly in terms of its content, these other categories of less-protected sexual speech are defined in substantial part by their context. In fact, two of them are defined in terms of contextual factors that—along with their sexual content—have repeatedly weighed in favor of reduced speech protection. The three categories are:

1. "Indecent" or "patently offensive" speech that is conveyed via over-the-air broadcast TV or radio (the Court has treated speech conveyed via broadcast as less

protected than the very same speech conveyed via other media),

2. Sexually suggestive speech during a high school assembly at which young teens are present (the Court has held that public schools may impose speech restrictions that would not be permissible in the general public sphere), and

3. "Adult" businesses, which may be subject to special zoning restrictions, in large part to locate them away from schools and other places where children are present.

What is the trend in the Court's most recent decisions about sexual expression?

The modern Court's general trajectory concerning sexual expression has been consistent with its overall general free speech trajectory: increasingly insisting on content neutrality. Almost all of the Court's decisions that have denied full First Amendment protection to certain subsets of sexual expression are about half a century old, dating back to the 1970s and 1980s. In more recent years, the Court has consistently rejected government arguments for expanding these existing subsets of less-protected sexual expression, and it has likewise rejected arguments for designating additional such subsets. For instance, the Court refused to extend the concept of illegal child pornography to images that look identical to it, but—crucially—did not use any actual minors in the production process. Similarly, the Court consistently has refused to permit the government to ban "indecent" or "patently offensive" expression in any other media, beyond the broadcast media. To the contrary, it has held that such expression is fully protected in all the other media on which it has ruled: telephone, cable TV, and the internet.

One reason for the Court's increasing protection of sexual expression is the absence of a bright-line distinction between such expression and the "political" speech that receives the strongest First Amendment protection. Much sexually themed speech touches on vital matters of public concern, involving major public policy debates. Consider, for example, speech about abortion, contraception, gender identity, LGBTQ+ rights, sexual assault, sexual harassment, sexually transmitted diseases, and women's rights.

As I have been writing this book (in 2022-23), state legislators and other officials in many states have sought to restrict multiple books in public and school libraries that were written by LGBTQ+ authors and/or feature LGBTQ+ characters, which were selected by professional librarians consistent with the educational and ethical standards of the library profession. Yet political critics have asserted that these books are "obscene" or "pornographic." There even have been attempts to criminally prosecute librarians for including such works in their collections, and to pass new state laws that facilitate such prosecutions. For example, bills that were introduced in the Indiana and Iowa legislatures in 2022 would criminalize as obscene even material that had "legitimate educational purposes." These efforts would violate the First Amendment, since they would outlaw speech that is not within the Supreme Court's definition of constitutionally unprotected obscenity; consistent with the special status of expression about matters of public concern, the obscenity definition does not extend to expression with "serious . . . value," such as material with "legitimate educational purposes."

How protected is "commercial" speech?

The Court has used the term "commercial speech" to refer to advertising and other speech about commercial transactions, although it has not delineated a specific definition of such expression. The Court's decisions about this content-defined category of speech, which long received no First Amendment protection, have evolved in the same increasingly speech-protective direction as its decisions about sexual expression. Until 1975, the Court treated commercial speech as categorically excluded from First Amendment protection, solely by virtue of its subject matter. In its milestone 1975 *Virginia v. Bigelow* ruling, though, the Court recognized that there is no clear distinction between the political speech that it has always considered supremely important and the commercial speech that it had traditionally deemed of lesser value.

Bigelow has recently gained renewed relevance, in light of the Court's June 2022 *Dobbs v. Jackson Women's Health Organization* decision overturning *Roe v. Wade*. The ad at issue in *Bigelow* advised women in Virginia, where abortion was then illegal, that they could receive abortions in New York, where they were legal. This is precisely the type of ad that we can anticipate in the wake of *Dobbs*. We can also anticipate the type of criminal prosecution that Virginia successfully brought against the newspaper editor of the Virginia "alternative newsweekly" that had published the ad. The Virginia Supreme Court had upheld the editor's criminal conviction under a state statute that made it a misdemeanor "to encourage or prompt the procuring of abortion," including "by advertisement." The Virginia Supreme Court rejected the publisher's First Amendment defense based on U.S. Supreme Court precedents that had denied First Amendment protection to paid commercial ads.[6]

After the 2022 *Dobbs* decision, the National Right to Life Committee circulated a model anti-abortion statute that parallels the Virginia statute in *Bigelow*; it outlaws "aiding and abetting" illegal abortions, and it defines "aiding and abetting" sufficiently broadly to include ads like the one in *Bigelow*. Therefore, current and future ads about abortion services, distributed in states where abortion is illegal, will depend upon the very same First Amendment principles that *Bigelow* enforced.

In *Bigelow*, the U.S. Supreme Court rejected former holdings that commercial speech was categorically excluded from First

Amendment protection, in part because such speech could not be clearly distinguished from political speech. Focusing on specific aspects of the particular ad at issue, the Court commented:

> The advertisement . . . did more than simply propose a commercial transaction. It . . . conveyed information of potential interest and value to a diverse audience—not only to readers possibly in need of the [abortion] services offered, but also to those with a general curiosity about . . . the subject matter, . . . and to readers seeking reform in Virginia.

Additionally, the Court observed, "the activity advertised pertained to constitutional interests," citing its 1973 *Roe* ruling.

Just one year after the 1975 *Bigelow* decision, the Court extended its protection of commercial speech even to the very kind of bare-bones ad that did *not* do "more than simply propose a commercial transaction"—in other words, offering to sell certain products or services at specified prices—which *Bigelow* had distinguished from the abortion services ad in that case. In further contrast with the *Bigelow* ad, this one did not "[pertain] to constitutional" interests such as reproductive freedom. In *Virginia State Board of Pharmacy v. Virginia Citizens Consumer Council*, the Court struck down a Virginia law barring any pharmacists' ads for prescription drugs that included the drugs' prices.

Notably, the lawsuit challenging the advertising ban in the *Virginia Citizens* case had been brought by consumer advocate Ralph Nader's then-newly-formed Public Citizen Litigation Group, which stressed that the ban violated consumers' right to receive information that they considered vitally important, in addition to violating the pharmacists' right to convey such information. It is also noteworthy that this decision was joined by all of the Court's liberal Justices, while conservative Justice

William Rehnquist was the only dissenter. I underscore these facts because some recent critics of strong First Amendment protection for commercial speech assume that this protection primarily benefits business interests, rather than the general public interest or individual consumers' interests. Consequently, it is important to examine *Virginia Citizens'* detailed explanation of the benefits that this First Amendment protection provides to consumers and to our economy and society more generally, as well as to pharmacists and other advertisers:

> [W]e may assume that the advertiser's interest is . . . purely economic. . . . That hardly disqualifies him from protection under the First Amendment. The interests of the contestants in a labor dispute are primarily economic, but it has long been settled that both the employee and the employer are protected by the First Amendment. . . . [A] . . . consumer's interest in the free flow of commercial information . . . may be as keen, if not keener by far, than his interest in the day's most urgent political debate. . . . So long as we preserve a predominantly free enterprise economy, the allocation of our resources in large measure will be made through numerous private economic decisions. It is a matter of public interest that those decisions, in the aggregate, be intelligent and well informed. To this end, the free flow of commercial information is indispensable. . . . [I]t is also indispensable to the formation of intelligent opinions as to how that system ought to be regulated or altered. Therefore, even if the First Amendment were thought to be primarily an instrument to enlighten public decisionmaking in a democracy, we could not say that the free flow of [commercial] information does not serve that goal.

Notwithstanding the Court's recognition that commercial speech addresses matters of public concern, a factor that weighs in favor of strong First Amendment protection, commercial speech restrictions are not subject to the same demanding "strict scrutiny" test that generally applies to content-based speech restrictions. Instead, the Court subjects commercial speech restrictions to the less demanding "intermediate scrutiny" test, under which the government must show only that the restriction "substantially" promotes a "significant" government interest, in contrast with strict scrutiny's required showing that the restriction is "necessary"/"the least restrictive alternative" to promote a government interest of "compelling importance." The Court has said that commercial speech warrants only this lesser degree of protection because commercial speech "occurs in an area traditionally subject to government regulation." Although some Justices have urged that commercial speech restrictions should be subject to strict scrutiny, the Court has not deemed it necessary to resolve that issue, having repeatedly struck down commercial speech restrictions even under the less-demanding intermediate scrutiny.

In a 2001 concurring opinion, Justice Thomas suggested that even restrictions on advertising harmful products, such as tobacco products, to minors should be limited to the same narrow concept of punishable incitement applicable to other expression—including classic political speech—that potentially induces other harmful conduct. In both situations, he emphasized, the expression seeks to persuade the listener to engage in harmful conduct, whether consuming tobacco or adopting and acting upon anti-democratic or racist ideology. He wrote:

Calls for limits on expression always are made when the specter of some threatened harm is looming. The identity of the harm may vary. People will be inspired by totalitarian dogmas and subvert the Republic. They will be inflamed by racial demagoguery and embrace hatred and bigotry. Or they will be enticed by cigarette advertisements and choose to smoke, risking disease. It is therefore no answer for the State to say that the makers of cigarettes are doing harm: perhaps they are. But in that respect they are no different from the purveyors of other harmful products, or the advocates of harmful ideas. When the State seeks to silence them, they are all entitled to the protection of the First Amendment.

The fact that commercial speech is typically (although not exclusively) engaged in by profit-seeking business enterprises cannot justify relegating it to reduced First Amendment protection. The Court explained this conclusion in its 1952 decision overturning the 1915 decision that had denied First Amendment protection for movies on the ground that "the exhibition of moving pictures is a business." In unanimously reversing that ruling, the Court explained:

> It is urged that motion pictures do not fall within the First Amendment's aegis because their production, distribution, and exhibition is a large-scale business conducted for private profit. We cannot agree. That books, newspapers, and magazines are published and sold for profit does not prevent them from being a form of expression whose liberty is safeguarded by the First Amendment.

How is First Amendment analysis affected by the communications medium?

The First Amendment itself expressly protects the freedom of both "speech" and "press." When it was ratified, there were no other communications media. Although the Court has construed the First Amendment as extending to all new communications media that have been invented since then, it also has said that the communications medium by which speech is transmitted is a factor affecting the extent of that speech's protection. Historically, print expression has been the most protected and broadcast the least protected.

More recently, the communications medium by which speech is transmitted has become a less significant factor in determining how much protection the speech should receive, thus paralleling the diminishing importance of the content factors addressed above. Nonetheless, the medium continues to play some role in the Court's analysis in one key respect. The Court still permits government to restrict "patently offensive" or "indecent" speech that is transmitted via over-the-air broadcast, even though it fully protects that very same speech when transmitted via any other medium: print, telephone, cable, or internet. The Court's dated decisions relegating broadcast expression to less-protected status were based on the following factors: "the history of extensive Government regulation of the broadcast medium . . .; the scarcity of available frequencies at its inception . . .; and its invasive nature."

In 1997, when the Court first considered the extent to which online expression should receive First Amendment protection, it concluded that "none of [the] factors" that had supported broadcast regulation "are . . . present in cyberspace." For example, it contrasted online expression with broadcast expression in terms of the degree of user control. The Court characterized members of the broadcast audience as passive—and at least in some cases unwilling—recipients of expression that is thrust upon them in an "invasive" fashion, whereas internet users affirmatively seek out expressive content. For these reasons, the Court explained, online expression was not governed by its earlier decisions that upheld restrictions on "patently offensive" or "indecent" broadcast expression, in order to shield audience members who might prefer not to see it—in particular, to assist parents who seek to shield their children from such expression. In contrast, the Court determined that this rationale does not apply to the internet, because of the unlikelihood that any user will be unwittingly exposed to any expression. The Court also has distinguished broadcast expression from expression on the internet and other media in additional respects, including the availability of less speech-restrictive alternative measures, facilitating parents' blocking of their own children's access through various filtering technologies.

The Court's broadcast cases remain in force despite the following critiques:

- Their reasoning has been faulted ever since they were issued, including by Justices all across the Court's ideological spectrum.
- They were issued decades ago (in the 1960s and 1970s) and have not been recently reexamined.
- They have fallen increasingly out of step with the overall speech-protective evolution of the Court's rulings regarding all other media.
- They have also increasingly fallen out of step with technological developments, including the convergence among formerly distinct media.

I can illustrate the anomalous nature of the ongoing broadcast restrictions through my own experience as a free speech educator. When I am interviewed on broadcast television about one of the most important Supreme Court free speech decisions, which overturned a young man's Vietnam-era conviction for wearing a jacket with the message "Fuck the Draft," that crucial word "Fuck" is bleeped out; otherwise, the broadcaster could incur a fine of up to $325,000 for each utterance of the word, and an increased risk that its broadcast license would not be renewed. In contrast, the very same interview, viewed on the very same TV screen, will remain unexpurgated and unpunished if it is transmitted via cable or internet.

In several recent cases, broadcasters have urged the Supreme Court to revisit and overturn its dated, controversial rulings that permit such strict broadcast regulation, but the Court has declined to address that issue.

How is First Amendment analysis affected by where the expression takes place—that is, on what type of government property?

This "place" factor applies to speech that is conveyed not via a communications medium, but rather, in person—for example, via talking, leafletting, or picketing. It focuses on the particular type of government or public property where the expression is taking place. (Because of the state action doctrine, private-property owners have no First Amendment obligation to permit expressive activities on their property.)

For purposes of assessing what speech restrictions are permissible on particular types of public property, the Court has classified all such property into three categories of "public forums": "traditional public forums," "limited public forums," and "non-public forums." Traditional public forums are streets, parks, and sidewalks, which traditionally have been open to the general public for expressive activities. Limited public forums constitute other types of public property, which the government chooses to make available for speech that is limited in terms of the speakers who have access to it and/or the topics they may address. Although these kinds of public property have specific primary purposes, opening them for limited free speech purposes is not incompatible with those primary purposes. For example, public schools and libraries often make meeting rooms available to the general public during times when those rooms are not needed to serve the schools' and libraries' primary functions. School and library officials could well limit these facilities to community members, or to certain topics. For instance, a school could choose to make its meeting rooms available only to students, and only for studying or working on school-related projects. Non-public forums constitute types of government property whose primary purpose the Court deems incompatible with any free speech access for members of the general public, even when limited to certain categories of speakers and/or topics. Classic examples are prisons and military facilities.[7]

Government may never enforce viewpoint-based regulations on any public property. Even in a limited public forum, the government may limit the subjects that are discussed, but not the viewpoints. In the hypothetical example cited above, a public school could create a limited public forum that was available only for student discussion of topics related to the school curriculum or extracurricular activities, but it could not limit the viewpoints that students could express about those topics.

How is First Amendment analysis affected by the speaker's identity or role?

The 2010 *Citizens United* case, which upheld certain First Amendment rights for corporations (both for-profit and not-for-profit) and unions, is based in part on the following rationale: that speech restrictions disfavoring particular speakers are as constitutionally problematic as speech restrictions disfavoring particular content or topics. In some earlier cases, *Citizens United* recognized, the Court had held that some people have only reduced free speech rights in certain contexts: namely, public school students, prisoners, military personnel, and government employees. Crucially, though, while these diminished free speech rights "operate to the disadvantage of certain persons," they do not flow from the speakers' identities, considered alone. Rather, as *Citizens United* pointed out, such lessened free speech rights result from another factor that critically affects the free speech analysis: in what capacity the government is acting and, correspondingly, the role that the individual is playing in that particular context. When government acts not in its role as the general regulator of the public sphere, but instead in another role—for example, as an employer that is regulating the workplace conduct of its employees—it may impose more speech restrictions, in order to effectively carry out its responsibilities in that role. In short, a government employer may impose a certain speech restriction on someone who is acting in her capacity as a government employee, even though the very same speech restriction would be unconstitutional if the government imposed it on the very same person in her capacity as a member of the community at large (i.e., while not on the job).

How is First Amendment analysis affected by the type of regulation?

In addition to the above-discussed factors concerning the nature of the speech that is being regulated—its content, its medium of communication or the place where it occurs, and the speaker's identity/role—another major factor that affects First Amendment analysis is the nature of the regulation.

What First Amendment standards govern content-based regulations?

Content-based speech restrictions constitute the most dangerous form of censorship, because they "raise the specter that the Government may effectively drive certain ideas or viewpoints from the marketplace." Therefore, content-based regulations are presumptively unconstitutional, and will be deemed constitutional only if the government can satisfy a heavy burden of proof to justify them. Under the "strict scrutiny" test, a court will closely examine the regulation, and uphold it only if the government can demonstrate that the regulation is necessary to promote a goal or purpose of "compelling" importance. While the government usually can easily satisfy the purpose prong of the strict scrutiny test—by showing, for instance, that it aims to promote goals such as public health or safety, or other constitutional rights, including equality rights—it is much harder for government to satisfy the test's necessary prong. To satisfy this requirement, the government must show not only that the regulation does materially promote the government's purpose, but also that it is "the least restrictive alternative" means for doing so—in other words, that no less speech-suppressive measure would effectively do so.

Upon close examination, many speech restrictions, no matter how well intended to advance important goals, cannot be shown even to effectively advance those goals, let alone to constitute the least speech-restrictive means for doing so. To cite one example, this is the reason why the Supreme Court struck down two federal statutes outlawing "indecent" and "patently offensive" online speech accessible to children, whose stated purpose was to protect children's well-being. Even assuming that this purpose was sufficiently important (the Court did not need to resolve this issue, and hence did not do so), the Court reasoned that the speech restrictions were not the least restrictive means to promote it. Rather, the Court elaborated, parents who wanted to shield their own children from certain material could do so with parental-control measures on their own home computers. Under such an approach, the targeted expression would remain available for adults, as well as for minors whose parents did not choose to shield them from it.

These internet decisions follow the pattern of several earlier rulings, also enforcing the least restrictive alternative principle, in which the Court likewise struck down child-protective censorship measures that also deprived adults of the same material. The Court repeatedly has held that no matter how important it might be to shield children from certain expressive materials, depriving adults of access to those materials is never a permissible means for pursuing that end, because it fails the necessary/least restrictive alternative test. For instance, in cases striking down restrictions on adult access to "indecent" or "patently offensive" telephone and cable communications, which had been premised on the child-protection rationale, the Court said that "the Government may not [reduce] the adult population . . . to . . . only what is fit for children."

What First Amendment standards govern content-neutral regulations?

Content-neutral speech restrictions are often referred to as "time, place, and manner" regulations, because they limit when, where, and how the speech occurs. For instance, as a 1949 Supreme Court decision recognized, a content-neutral regulation could bar sound trucks from blaring their messages in residential neighborhoods at times when most residents are sleeping; such a bar would apply evenhandedly to any and all expression, regardless of its topic or perspective. Along with restrictions that comply with the emergency principle, content-neutral restrictions also present "no realistic" risk that government is "[suppressing] . . . ideas."

Content-neutral speech restrictions do, though, pose another significant First Amendment danger: that government will make it too hard to convey *any* ideas. Even if *all* ideas are equally stifled, this is still a threat to both individual liberty and democratic self-government. For this reason, the Court sensibly requires government to vindicate content-neutral regulations by showing (among other things) that there are "ample alternative channels" for speakers to convey their messages—that is, at other times, in other places, and/or in other manners.

Government bears the burden of proof to justify content-neutral regulations, just as it does regarding content-based regulations. Although the applicable "intermediate scrutiny" test is less demanding than the "strict scrutiny" that applies to content-based regulations (as the labels clearly denote), government nevertheless often fails to satisfy it. Under intermediate scrutiny, the government must show not only the "ample alternative channels" referenced above, but also that the speech restriction "substantially" promotes a goal of "significant" importance, and is "narrowly tailored" to do so. As is the case under strict scrutiny, the government generally can satisfy intermediate scrutiny's purpose prong, but it is harder for the government to satisfy the other elements of the test. Government often fails to show that the restriction actually is effective in promoting its purpose and that it is "narrowly tailored"—in other words, that it does not "burden substantially more speech than necessary to further the government's" interests.

One noteworthy example of content-neutral regulations that courts regularly have struck down are regulations that many colleges and universities have adopted, which confine leafletting, picketing, and all other expressive activities on their campuses to small, inconveniently located (and ironically named) "free speech zones." Reviewing courts have consistently concluded that these regulations do not satisfy the intermediate scrutiny standard, because they are not narrowly tailored, and do not leave open ample alternative channels for expressive activity.

To illustrate content-neutral restrictions that do satisfy intermediate scrutiny, I will cite a situation of special current interest as I'm writing this passage: protests outside the homes of Supreme Court Justices who voted in the 2022 *Dobbs* decision to overturn *Roe v. Wade*. Would a content-neutral time, place, or manner restriction on residential picketing survive the applicable intermediate scrutiny? The Supreme Court answered that question in the affirmative in its 1988 *Frisby v. Schultz* decision—so long as the restriction barred only picketing that solely targeted a single residence. In contrast, the Court stressed, the law in *Frisby* did allow picketing in the general neighborhood—indeed even picketing focused on the single block in which the targeted residence was located. Given its limited scope, the Court reasoned, this residential picketing ban satisfied both the narrow tailoring and ample alternative channels elements of intermediate scrutiny. First, the ban on single-residence picketing was narrowly tailored to protect the vital interest in residential privacy, which earlier cases had recognized as uniquely important. In a 1980 case, for example, the Court had said that "the home becomes something less than a home [during] . . . picketing . . . . [The] tensions and pressures may be psychological, not physical, but they are not, for that reason, less inimical to family privacy and truly domestic tranquility." Just as the regulation's focus on individual homes satisfied the narrow tailoring requirement, by the same token it left open ample alternative channels for the demonstrators' expression. The Court laid these out: "Protestors . . . may enter [residential] neighborhoods, alone or in groups, even marching. . . . They may go door-to-door to proselytize their views. They may distribute literature in this manner . . . or through the mails. They may contact residents by telephone."

Whatever your own views may be about *Roe* and *Dobbs*, *Frisby* illustrates yet again why we must all defend "freedom for the thought that we hate" if we are to enjoy freedom for the thought that we love. Specifically, *Frisby* involved a factual situation that was the obverse of the post-*Dobbs* scenario. The residential picketing restriction in *Frisby* had been enacted to curb such picketing by anti–abortion-rights demonstrators outside the home of a doctor who performed abortions. Just as *Frisby* allowed anti–abortion-rights demonstrators to picket on the block where the doctor lived—although not solely in front of his house—it also allows pro–abortion-rights demonstrators to picket on the block where Justice Samuel Alito (*Dobbs*'s author) lives, but not solely in front of his house.

What First Amendment standards govern prior restraints?

Along with content-based restrictions, "prior restraints" constitute another type of speech regulation that the Court has held to be presumptively unconstitutional. Indeed, it has said that "[a]ny system of prior restraints of expression comes to this Court bearing a heavy presumption against its constitutional validity, pronouncing such restraints "the most serious and least tolerable infringement on First Amendment rights."

While it is clear that the Court will almost automatically strike down any speech regulation that it classifies as a prior restraint, it is far from clear which speech regulations the Court will classify as such. Rather than providing a definition, the Court has proceeded in its customary common-law, case-specific fashion. Berkeley Law School Dean Erwin Chemerinsky's constitutional law treatise summarized the case law as follows: "In practice, most prior restraints involve either an administrative rule requiring some form of license or permit before one may engage in expression, or a judicial order directing an individual not to engage in expression, on pain of contempt." I will briefly elaborate on both common types of constitutionally suspect prior restraints.

When the First Amendment was adopted, the requirement of securing a government license as a prerequisite for publication was generally considered the most egregious violation of the freedoms of speech and press. The modern Court permits licensing-type requirements, including parade permits, only if they comply with three criteria:

1. There must be an important reason for the licensing. For example, parade permit requirements ensure that any parade route is used by only one group at a time and that there is adequate police protection.
2. The standards for issuing the license must be clear, leaving almost no discretion to the licensing authority. Along with other First Amendment rules that constrain government discretion, the purpose is to ensure that officials are pursuing viewpoint-neutral goals such as crowd control, and not disfavoring certain speakers or messages.
3. There must be procedural safeguards, including prompt judicial review of any license denial.

The second of the two most common types of prior restraint, a court order barring speech, is illustrated by the famous 1971 "Pentagon Papers case." Both the *New York Times* and the *Washington Post* had published, and were planning on continuing to publish, excerpts from a top-secret Pentagon report about U.S. involvement in Vietnam, which had been leaked by the whistle-blower Daniel Ellsberg. The Nixon administration filed lawsuits seeking to block the publications, arguing that they would adversely impact the United States' ongoing Vietnam War efforts and other national security interests. Reviewing the case in record-breaking time, thus underscoring its urgency, the Supreme Court rejected the administration's arguments, concluding that the government "had not met" its "heavy burden of showing justification" for the injunctions. Although six Justices joined in that conclusion, there was no majority opinion with explanatory rationales and analysis. Each of these six Justices, as well as the three dissenting Justices, wrote a separate opinion, stressing different rationales.

One striking common theme emerges across the various opinions in the Pentagon Papers case. Three of the Justices in the majority, as well as all three dissenters, concurred that the publication of the Pentagon Papers could well substantially damage U.S. national security interests, yet the Court still concluded that the First Amendment barred the prior restraint. I hasten to note that all of the information that later came to light, after the litigation, made clear that there actually was nothing in the Pentagon Papers that would have jeopardized national security; the government's claims and fears in that vein were greatly exaggerated, as top Nixon administration officials later admitted. But the Justices didn't know that. They hadn't actually reviewed the whole massive document, so they could not conclusively discredit the government's assertions about the serious harms that publication would cause. That said, the Justices also could not conclusively credit the government's assertions. As Justice Brennan's opinion put it:

The entire thrust of the Government's claim throughout these cases has been that publication of the material sought to be enjoined "could," or "might," or "may" prejudice the national interest in various ways. But the

First Amendment tolerates absolutely no prior judicial restraints of the press predicated upon surmise or conjecture that untoward consequences may result.

Weighing against the dire—albeit ultimately unsubstantiated —government claims about the potential dangers of permitting publication, the majority Justices stressed the actual dangers of barring publication through a court-ordered prior restraint. For example, Justice Hugo Black wrote: "The Government's power to censor the press was abolished so that the press would remain forever free to censure the Government. . . . Only [an] . . . unrestrained press can effectively expose deception in government." And the opinion of Judge Murray Gurfein, the federal trial court judge who rejected the government's effort to bar the *New York Times'* continued publication, made the important point that national security would be undermined—not advanced—by such a prior restraint. Notably, before his judicial appointment, Murray Gurfein had significant national security experience, including through service as a Lieutenant Colonel in the U.S. Army's Office of Strategic Services. He eloquently wrote:

> The security of the Nation is not at the ramparts alone. Security also lies in the value of our free institutions. A cantankerous press, an obstinate press, a ubiquitous press must be suffered by those in authority to preserve the even greater values of freedom of expression and the right of the people to know.

What First Amendment standards govern whether a regulation's language is too "broad" or "vague"?

In addition to the substantive nature of a speech regulation (i.e., what its impact is on the targeted expression), another aspect of a speech regulation that also affects First Amendment analysis is how it is formulated. The primary concern is to avoid language that is either "substantially overbroad" or "unduly vague," hence suppressing even more speech than what the regulation seeks to target. The adverbs "substantially" and "unduly" recognize that, given language's inevitable imprecision, any regulation will likely be at least somewhat overbroad and vague; the First Amendment bars only pronounced degrees of overbreadth and vagueness.

A "substantially overbroad" law encompasses a substantial amount of constitutionally protected expression, as well as constitutionally unprotected expression. For instance, in a 2012 case, the Supreme Court struck down a federal statute on this ground even though the statute aimed to suppress some expression that is not constitutionally protected: intentional lies about having received military honors, resulting in a material benefit to the liar and harm to others—that is, a specific type of fraud. The statute's actual language, however, was much more sweeping, extending even to negligent misstatements in one-on-one personal conversations that had no tangible impact on anyone. Stressing that "some false statements are inevitable" in any "open and vigorous expression of views in public and private conversation," the Court noted that a purported government power to punish false speech "absent any evidence that the speech was used to gain a material advantage" would have "no clear limiting principle," but could extend to "an endless list of subjects." Referring to George Orwell's dystopian novel *1984*, the Court said that "our constitutional tradition stands against the idea that we need Oceania's Ministry of Truth." After the Court struck down that statute on overbreadth grounds, Congress passed a revised version that was narrowly formulated to outlaw only constitutionally unprotected lies about military honors, consistent with the general concept of constitutionally unprotected fraud: lies that were made with the intent to obtain money, property, or other tangible benefits.

The Supreme Court has held that any law is "unduly vague," and hence unconstitutional, when people "of common intelligence must necessarily guess at its meaning." Any overly vague law violates tenets of "due process" or fairness, as well as equality, because it is inherently susceptible to arbitrary and discriminatory enforcement. When an unduly vague law regulates speech in particular, the law also violates the First Amendment, because it deters people from engaging in constitutionally protected speech for fear that they might run afoul of the law. Unduly vague speech restrictions vest enforcing officials with excessive discretion, which they will foreseeably exercise in accordance with their own subjective values, or those of powerful community factions. At best, officials will enforce such laws in an arbitrary and capricious manner; at worst, officials will enforce such laws in a discriminatory manner, selectively suppressing disfavored viewpoints and speakers, and thus violating the cardinal viewpoint- and speaker-neutrality principles. For these reasons, the Supreme Court has enforced the "void for vagueness" doctrine with special strictness concerning laws that regulate speech.

Many U.S. colleges and universities have enacted what are colloquially called "hate speech codes," which regulate certain speech conveying discriminatory messages, on the rationale that the speech constitutes discriminatory "harassment," "fighting words," or other contextually defined punishable speech. (Any regulation of such speech based solely on disfavor or generalized fear of its message would be squarely unconstitutional, violating the viewpoint-neutrality and emergency principles.) Yet reviewing courts have consistently struck down such codes on overbreadth and/or vagueness grounds, which are closely interrelated in many cases. By failing to clearly define the forbidden, constitutionally unprotected speech—and thus sweeping in much constitutionally protected speech—the typical campus speech codes have violated both the vagueness and overbreadth doctrines, with an enormous chilling impact on campus speech. To illustrate these intertwined problems, I will quote the 2021 federal appellate court decision that points to both problems with the University of Central Florida's "discriminatory harassment" policy. The court helpfully provided a detailed analysis of just some of the policy's problematic, speech-suppressing language (which is all too typical of these kinds of campus codes).

[W]hat does it mean for one student's speech to "unreasonably . . . alter" another student's educational experience? Both terms—"unreasonably" and "alter"—are pretty amorphous, [and] their application would likely vary from one student to another. . . . At oral argument, we asked the University's lawyer . . . whether particular statements would violate the discriminatory-harassment policy: (1) "abortion is immoral"; (2) "unbridled open immigration is a danger to America on a variety of levels"; and (3) "the Palestinian movement is anti-semitic." To his considerable credit—but to the policy's considerable discredit—he candidly acknowledged that while "it d[id] not sound to [him]" like the speech would be proscribed under the policy, he couldn't say for sure. . . . If UCF's own attorney . . . can't tell whether a particular statement would violate the policy, it seems eminently fair to conclude that the school's students can't either.

It is especially noteworthy that vagueness and/or overbreadth problems have plagued campus hate speech codes in particular, since many of these codes have been drafted with the assistance of faculty experts on their campuses, including leading First Amendment scholars. Therefore, the codes' failure to comply with the governing constitutional standards hardly reflects ignorance of those standards; rather, it indicates that the problem lies in the speech that is targeted for restriction—that is, speech with controversial content, and not speech that has a tight, direct causal connection to harm. This persistent problem was underscored by Eleanor Holmes Norton, a Black civil rights lawyer who was the first woman to chair the Equal Employment Opportunity Commission, and who has been the longtime District of Columbia Representative in Congress, as well as a faculty member at Georgetown Law School. Referring to campus hate speech codes, she said: "It is technically impossible to write an anti-speech code that cannot be twisted against speech nobody means to bar. It has been tried and tried and tried."

What context-defined categories of speech may be punished, consistent with the viewpoint-neutrality and emergency principles?

The Supreme Court has delineated the context-based criteria for several categories of speech that satisfy the emergency principle. While such speech does contain specific content, it may not be punished based solely on the disfavored nature of its content or viewpoint. For example, for speech to be punishable as fraud, it must not only be a false statement of fact, but additionally the speaker must have known that it was false and intended the listener to rely on it, and the listener must actually have relied on it and consequently suffered demonstrable tangible harm, such as financial injury. In parallel fashion, certain false statements are punishable as defamation only when they injure someone's reputation and cause demonstrable harm, such as financial injury. Other contextually defined categories of punishable speech, which also comport with the general emergency principle (and hence with the complementary viewpoint neutrality principle),[8] are listed here in alphabetical order: bribery, child pornography, crime-facilitating speech, extortion, "fighting words," harassment, intentional incitement, perjury, and "true threats."

Under what context-defined speech categories may government punish certain hate speech?

By way of illustration, I will set out the context-specific criteria that the Court has laid out for six categories of speech that comply with the emergency principle. I have chosen to focus on six categories that apply to specific instances of "hate speech"—speech that conveys hateful, discriminatory views. Given the understandably great public concern about such speech, it is important for readers to realize that it may be punished in multiple contexts, when it satisfies the emergency principle by directly causing or threatening serious imminent harm. Consistent with the viewpoint-neutrality principle, such speech could not be punished solely because its message is disfavored. Nonetheless, particular instances of hate speech, considered in their overall context, may well be subject to punishment when they satisfy the context-specific criteria for crime-facilitating speech, fighting words, targeted harassment, hostile environment harassment, intentional incitement, and true threats.

What is constitutionally unprotected crime-facilitating expression?

Government may punish expression that directly, imminently facilitates specific crimes against specific individuals. One example is the *fatwa* against Salman Rushdie and others associated with the publication and distribution of *The Satanic Verses*; it constitutes a punishable solicitation of specific crimes against specific individuals. Other examples include communications that intentionally provide essential information for carrying out illegal acts. One notorious instance occurred during the 1994 Rwandan genocide, in which some members of the ethnic majority Hutus slaughtered an estimated 500,000 to 800,000 members of the Tutsi ethnic minority. The government radio station RTLM (Radio Television des Mille Collines), which was owned and controlled by Hutu hard-liners, provided essential information that facilitated the murders of specific Tutsis. Article 19, the London-based international free speech organization (whose name derives from the speech-protecting provision in the Universal Declaration of Human Rights), described RTLM's role as having "organised" genocide, "notably by identifying targets . . . [and] refuges where potential victims were hiding."[9]

What is constitutionally unprotected intentional incitement?

In everyday speech, we use the term "incitement" quite loosely, to describe expression that might induce those to whom it is communicated to commit a violent or otherwise illegal act. In contrast, in the landmark 1969 *Brandenburg v. Ohio* case, the Supreme Court unanimously ruled that speech constitutes constitutionally punishable incitement only if the speaker intentionally incites imminent violent or otherwise illegal conduct that is likely to occur immediately. The Court consequently held that the First Amendment protected the following statements that a Ku Klux Klan leader made at a rally of his followers, since they did not satisfy these criteria: "I believe the Nigger should be returned to Africa, the Jew returned to Israel. . . . [I]f our [government] continues to suppress the white, Caucasian race, it's possible that there might have to be some revengeance [*sic*] taken."

The Court enforced this narrow concept of punishable incitement 13 years later in *Claiborne Hardware v. NAACP.* NAACP field organizer Charles Evers had used threatening, violent language to deter violation of an NAACP-organized boycott of racially discriminatory white businesses. Several Black people who violated the boycott were subsequently subject to violence, but the Court held that Evers's words did not constitute punishable incitement because the violent acts occurred weeks or months later, so the critical "imminency" standard was not satisfied.

Although the current concept of punishable incitement is appropriately strict, it may well be satisfied by hate speech in certain circumstances. A 1993 Supreme Court case, *Wisconsin v. Mitchell*, affords an example. It involved a group of young Black men who were discussing a scene from the 1988 movie "Mississippi Burning," which is about the 1960s civil rights movement. The scene showed a white man beating up a young Black boy who was praying. Enraged by this scene, one of the Black men, Todd Mitchell, asked the others, "Do you all feel hyped up to move on some white people?" Soon after, a white boy approached the group on the opposite side of the street where they were standing. As the boy walked by, Mitchell said to his companions: "You all want to fuck somebody up? There goes a white boy; go get him." Mitchell counted to three and pointed in the boy's direction. The group ran toward the boy and beat him severely. The boy was rendered unconscious and remained in a coma for four days. Although the Supreme Court upheld the conviction on a different rationale,[10] Mitchell's speech clearly satisfied the punishable incitement standard.

What are constitutionally unprotected fighting words?

Under modern First Amendment law, punishable fighting words constitute a specific type of punishable incitement: when speakers intentionally incite imminent violence against themselves (in contrast with third parties), through a face-to-face personal insult or provocation to fight that directly targets another person, and which is intended and likely to provoke an immediate violent reaction by that person.

In the 1942 *Chaplinsky* case, before the modern Court adopted this current limited concept of punishable fighting words, the Court upheld a fighting words conviction based on the since-repudiated bad tendency rationale that it endorsed at that time. *Chaplinsky* held that punishable "fighting words" include any words that "tend to incite an immediate breach of the peace." The "fighting words" that led to the criminal conviction in *Chaplinsky* included the speaker's denunciation of the law enforcement officer who arrested him, a typical situation in fighting words cases; the speaker had called the officer "a damned Fascist."

Although the Court has never overturned *Chaplinsky*, it has issued many subsequent speech-protective decisions that are inconsistent with *Chaplinsky*, and it has squarely rejected the general bad tendency concept that undergirded *Chaplinsky*. Not surprisingly, therefore, the Court has struck down every single one of the multiple post-*Chaplinsky* fighting words convictions it has reviewed. The Court consistently rejected the fighting words rationale as the asserted justification for punishing speech in a series of cases during the late 1960s and early 1970s, in which it overturned criminal convictions of Black people for expression protesting racial injustice and police abuse, including language protesting their arrests. The speakers had been charged under broad, vague laws proscribing offenses such as breach of the peace, disorderly conduct, or criminal mischief. In all of these cases, the Court distinguished *Chaplinsky* and narrowly construed the concept of constitutionally unprotected fighting words, as delineated above. To illustrate this pattern, I will briefly describe two of these cases.

In 1969, the Court overturned the malicious mischief conviction of Sidney Street, a Black decorated World War II veteran who had burned his own American flag on a street corner after learning about the shooting of James Meredith, the first Black student whom the racially segregated University of Mississippi had admitted, under pressure from the federal government. As his flag burned, Street said: "We don't need no damn flag . . . If they let that happen to Meredith we don't need an American flag." The Court explained: "[W]e cannot say that [Street's] remarks were so inherently inflammatory as to come within that small class of `fighting words' which are likely to provoke the average person to retaliation, and thereby cause a breach of the peace."

In a 1972 case, a middle-aged woman, Mrs. Mallie Lewis, was convicted for breach of the peace based on her statements to a police officer about her young son's arrest, which had just occurred. She and her husband were in their pickup truck following the police patrol car that was taking their son to a police station after his arrest. Officer Berner, who was in another patrol car, intercepted and stopped the truck, and asked Mr. Lewis for his driver's license. According to Officer Berner's testimony, which the trial judge accepted as true, Mrs. Lewis "started yelling and screaming that I had her son or did something to her son and she wanted to know where he was. . . . She said, 'you god damn m. f. police—I am going to [the Superintendent of Police] about this.'" Both Mr. and Mrs. Lewis testified to a very different version of Mrs. Lewis's statements, which the trial judge did not accept as true.[11] Nonetheless, even assuming (hypothetically) that Mrs. Lewis had made the statements that Officer Berner ascribed to her, the Supreme Court overturned her conviction because it was based on a New Orleans ordinance that outlawed speech far beyond constitutionally unprotected fighting words, making it unlawful "to curse or revile or to use obscene or opprobrious language toward or with reference to" a police officer performing his/her duties.

Justice Powell's concurring opinion in the *Lewis* case pointed to the pattern alluded to above: that many arrests in fighting words cases are made by police officers who claim that the people they are arresting utter the allegedly punishable language in protesting the arrests. As Powell observed, "the only witnesses are the arresting officer and the person charged. All that is required for conviction is that the court accept the [officer's] testimony." The facts of the *Lewis* case, he said, "well illustrate the possibility of abuse." Powell also cited the American Law Institute's 1961 recommendation that the fighting words doctrine should not apply to words uttered to law enforcement officials, since "a properly trained officer may reasonably be expected to exercise a higher degree of restraint than the average citizen, and thus be less likely to respond belligerently to" such words.

Although the current fighting words standard is as strict as the current general standard for punishable incitement, of which it now constitutes a subcategory, that standard could be satisfied by certain hate speech—for instance, if a member of the Ku Klux Klan personally insults a Black Lives Matter activist with face-to-face racist epithets, or vice versa. Multiple lower-court cases have held that directing the N-word toward a Black person, in various contexts that evidenced an intent and likelihood to provoke retaliatory violence, constituted punishable fighting words. For example, in 1997, the North Carolina Supreme Court stated that "[n]o fact is more generally known than that a white man who calls a black man a 'nigger' within his hearing will hurt and anger the black man, and often provoke him to confront the white man and retaliate."

What is constitutionally unprotected targeted harassment?

The government may punish expression that directly targets an individual or small group of individuals in a manner that, under all the facts and circumstances, unduly intrudes upon the targeted individuals' freedom or privacy. A classic example would be repeated unwanted telephone calls in the middle of the night, thus disturbing the targeted individual's privacy and rest. Such expression is punishable regardless of its viewpoint; the phone calls would be equally intrusive whether they conveyed messages of hate or love.[12] More recently, laws against such targeted harassment have been designated by other terms, including "anti-stalking" or "anti-bullying," but whatever the label, they outlaw the same range of expressive (and non-expressive) conduct, in a viewpoint-neutral manner.

As is always the case concerning free speech rights (and wrongs), the proverbial "devil"—or angel—"is in the details," turning on how a particular anti-harassment law is written and enforced. For example, in 2012, a proposed Arizona anti-harassment law would have made it a crime "for any person, with intent to . . . harass, annoy or offend, to use any electronic . . . device and use any obscene, lewd or profane language." This overly broad and vague language, which would encompass substantial protected speech, prompted criticism and redrafting. As enacted, the law was limited to speech that was directed to the person whom the speaker intended to harass, and threatened physical harm, or consisted of "anonymous, unwanted or unsolicited electronic communications" that disturbed the recipient's "peace, quiet or right of privacy."

What is constitutionally unprotected hostile environment harassment?

"Hostile environment" harassment arises in settings where individuals are required to be: workplaces or educational institutions. The Supreme Court has ruled that workplace expression may be punished as hostile environment harassment if it is sufficiently "severe or pervasive to alter the conditions of [the victim's] employment and create an abusive working environment." The Court has ruled that expression may be punished as hostile environment harassment in educational contexts when it is "so severe, pervasive, and objectively offensive, that it effectively bars the victim's access . . . to an educational opportunity or benefit."

Even in an employment setting, the Court has indicated that "a mere offensive utterance" is unlikely to constitute hostile environment harassment. Moreover, given the special importance of free speech in educational settings, the Court has stressed that offensive expression alone usually will not give rise to a claim of hostile environment harassment in such settings. Generalizations aside, though, the fact-intensive nature of the hostile environment test means that in some situations, a court might well deem language alone—considered in the overall context—to create a hostile environment; indeed, in particular circumstances, courts have found that even a single racist epithet could suffice.

In a 2021 decision, the U.S. Court of Appeals for the Fifth Circuit reaffirmed a conclusion that it (and other appellate courts) had previously reached: that, in the workplace, even a single instance of a racial epithet might support a hostile environment harassment claim, if it was "sufficiently severe," taking into account "the totality of the circumstances." The 2021 case involved the N-word directed to a Black employee by his supervisor. (The appellate court did not conclude that this incident did constitute hostile environment harassment, but it rejected the employer's argument that it could not possibly rise to that level, and remanded the case to the lower court to evaluate all the "circumstances" and to make the final determination accordingly.) Other federal appellate courts have observed that "[p]erhaps no single act can more quickly 'alter the conditions of employment and create an abusive working environment'—i.e., the Supreme Court's definition of a hostile workplace—than the use of an unambiguously racial epithet such as [the N-word] by a supervisor in the presence of his subordinates."

The federal Equal Employment Opportunity Commission recently settled a case in which it charged that a company's Black employees had been subjected to a racially hostile work environment due to multiple incidents of racist hate speech: A noose was displayed at the worksite; derogatory racial language was used by a direct supervisor and a manager of these employees, including references to the Ku Klux Klan; and the employees had been targeted with racial insults.[13]

What are constitutionally unprotected true threats?

Government may constitutionally punish what the Court has labeled "true threats," to distinguish them from the broader connotations of the term "threat" in everyday usage. True threats are statements through which "the speaker means to communicate a serious expression of an intent to commit . . . unlawful violence to a particular individual or group of individuals" and, in consequence, the targeted individuals reasonably fear that violence. The speaker need not actually intend to commit the threatened violence, because the reasonable fear of such violence constitutes serious harm in itself, hampering the threatened person's freedoms of movement and speech. The 2017 Unite the Right demonstration in Charlottesville, Virginia, well illustrates the distinction between hate speech that may not be punished solely because of its hateful, hated content, and hate speech that may be punished because, in context, it constitutes a true threat. When the white supremacists marched while chanting racist slogans such as, "You will not replace us" and "Jews will not replace us," the slogans' abhorrent messages alone did not justify punishing the marchers; that would have violated the viewpoint-neutrality principle. However, when one considers the overall context, this expression posed true threats to the counterdemonstrators who ringed the Jefferson statue on the University of Virginia campus; hundreds of marchers surrounded the counterdemonstrators at a close range, while brandishing flaming tiki torches.

When may government punish intentionally targeted racist epithets?

For many people who advocate censoring or punishing "hate speech," the paradigmatic situation they have in mind is when speakers deliberately aim racist epithets at members of a racial minority group. This kind of intentionally targeted insulting, discriminatory expression is already subject to punishment under several of the legal theories summarized above: if it intentionally "harries" or annoys the targeted persons by intruding upon their privacy or freedom of movement, it constitutes punishable harassment; if it intentionally makes the targeted persons reasonably fear that they will be subject to violence, it constitutes a punishable "true threat" (even if the speaker didn't intend to carry out any violence); and if it intentionally provokes a retaliatory violent response, it constitutes punishable fighting words. Moreover, when such expression occurs in an employment or educational setting, it constitutes punishable hostile environment harassment if it is sufficiently "severe" or "pervasive" to "create an abusive working environment" or to "effectively [bar]" targeted persons' "access . . . to an educational opportunity or benefit."

Why may government indirectly punish hate speech, under hate crimes laws?

In addition to the multiple contexts in which First Amendment principles permit hate speech to be directly punished, it also may be indirectly punished when it constitutes evidence of a "hate crime" or "bias crime." These terms refer to acts that are independently punishable as crimes—that is, independent of any associated expression—such as assaults or vandalism, when the perpetrators intentionally select the victimized persons or property for discriminatory reasons.

On the rationale that these crimes cause additional harm both to the victims and to society, they are subject to enhanced punishment. In a typical case, the perpetrators' discriminatory selection of the crime victim is proven through hateful, discriminatory remarks that the perpetrators made in the course of committing the crime or immediately prior to it.

In its 1993 *Wisconsin v. Mitchell* ruling, the Supreme Court unanimously rejected a First Amendment challenge to Wisconsin's hate crime statute. On the one hand, the defendant plausibly argued, and the Wisconsin Supreme Court held (by a divided vote), that the added penalty constituted a "thought crime," punishing him for his hateful ideas and thus violating the viewpoint-neutrality principle. On the other hand, as all of the U.S. Supreme Court Justices concluded, one could view the statute as analogous to an antidiscrimination law, imposing the extra penalty for the defendant's intentional discrimination in selecting his crime victim.

Such an antidiscrimination conception of hate crime laws—which is better captured by the term "bias crimes"— is highlighted by considering laws that bar employment discrimination in the United States. In this country, the general legal standard is "employment at will"; an employer usually may make employment decisions, including hiring and firing, for any reason or no reason. Antidiscrimination laws constitute an exception to this general standard. If an employer's reason for not hiring someone, or for firing someone, consists of intentional discrimination based on race or some other illegitimate consideration, that is illegal. The Supreme Court repeatedly has rejected First Amendment challenges to such antidiscrimination laws; for example, it stated that Title VII, the federal statute that bars employment discrimination, is "a permissible content-neutral regulation of conduct." Since intentional discrimination can transform an employment action that would be completely legal into an illegal one, then it seems even clearer that intentional discrimination can elevate an already criminal act into a more serious one.

To ensure that bias crime laws actually punish the discriminatory selection of crime victims and not discriminatory thoughts, these laws must be written and enforced so that a defendant's expressive conduct will not be taken into consideration unless it has a sufficiently tight, direct nexus to the crime. For example, in the Wisconsin case itself, Todd Mitchell's racist statement was so closely, causally connected to the crime that it even satisfied the demanding test for punishable incitement.

5

SPEECH RESTRICTIONS THAT THE FIRST AMENDMENT BARS

Why does the First Amendment bar non-emergency restrictions on speech with controversial content?

Many people, including politicians, advocate restricting speech with specific types of content that they consider at least potentially harmful, beyond the context-based restrictions that the First Amendment permits. The types of speech that are most often targeted for these content-based restrictions are "hate speech," "pornography," "violent speech," "extremist" or "terrorist" speech, "disinformation" or "misinformation," "offensive" speech, "incivility," and "blasphemy." I put all of these terms in quotation marks to underscore that the Supreme Court never has provided a definition for any of them, precisely because the Court has steadfastly declined to recognize any of the designated content-based speech categories as deserving anything less than full-fledged First Amendment protection.[1] Furthermore, the Court has barred non-emergency restrictions on several additional categories of controversial speech content, as to which it has spelled out some specific guidelines for restrictions that are consistent with the emergency principle. These guidelines constrain regulations of speech that could provoke retaliatory violence against the speaker or the speaker's supporters, speech that causes emotional distress, and defamation against public officials and figures.

Along with speech containing any message or content, all speech with these controversial types of content may be subject to context-based restrictions consistent with the emergency principle: if, in particular contexts, it directly causes or threatens certain imminent specific harms. For instance, in certain circumstances, hate speech, offensive speech, terrorist/extremist speech, violent speech, and incivility might well constitute punishable fighting words, true threats, or incitement. In specific contexts, blasphemy, incivility, offensive speech, and pornography might well constitute punishable harassment; and disinformation/misinformation might well constitute punishable defamation or fraud. Accordingly, the precise question is not the one that is generally posed in public debates: Why does the First Amendment bar restrictions on speech with this controversial content? Rather, it is this: Why does the First Amendment bar *non-emergency* restrictions on speech with this controversial content?

What First Amendment flaws are shared by non-emergency restrictions on speech with various kinds of controversial content?

This important question was answered in detail early in this book, as one of the most common, most challenging questions about/arguments against free speech. Here I will just briefly summarize that preceding answer, by listing the shared First Amendment flaws of all non-emergency speech restrictions:

- They are unduly vague and substantially overbroad, thus vesting enforcing officials with essentially unfettered discretion, leading to enforcement that is arbitrary at best, discriminatory at worst.
- They do not have a sufficient net benefit in terms of reducing the targeted speech's harmful impact. Any benefits are substantially offset, if not even outweighed,

by their unintended (but predictable) costs: suppressing non-targeted, non-harmful speech, increasing attention to/sympathy for the targeted speech, and disproportionately silencing marginalized voices and views.

• There are alternative measures, which are less speech-restrictive, that would be at least as effective as the non-emergency restrictions, if not more so.

In answering the following specific questions about why the First Amendment bars non-emergency restrictions on speech with various kinds of controversial content, I will not repeat the preceding general analysis, but will simply stress here that it applies fully to all such speech.

Why does the First Amendment bar non-emergency restrictions on . . .

—Hate speech?

It is important to understand why hate speech laws are inherently likely to be enforced in ways that further entrench dominant political and societal groups, and that further disempower marginalized individuals and groups. This pattern is not a result of occasional "abuses" of the laws, but rather is the inevitable, systematic result of any *use* of such laws, given their irreducible vagueness, which means that they bestow largely unfettered discretion upon the officials who enforce them.

The term "hate speech" has been hurled at a seemingly endless array of speech with diverse and even opposing messages, linked only by the fact that the person using this epithet hates the speech's idea. For example, influential politicians have denounced Black Lives Matter expression as hate speech against white people and/or police officers (and also as extremist/terrorist speech and disinformation/misinformation). Others in turn denounce that very denunciation as hate speech. In short, for the proponents and opponents of BLM expression alike, one faction's cherished anti-hate speech is the other's reviled hate speech.

No matter how many synonyms hate speech laws invoke to try to circumscribe the inherently vague, broad, and manipulable concept at their heart—"hate"—these laws unavoidably vest largely unconstrained power in enforcing authorities. Even when such authorities act in utmost good faith, they cannot enforce these open-textured laws except in accordance with their own subjective values, or those of other people. As one would expect in a representative democracy where officials are (appropriately) accountable to their constituents, officials are likely to enforce these laws in accordance with the values of majoritarian, powerful interest groups.

Even when hate speech laws are enforced to punish speech of avowed racists, they have not been shown to effectively reduce intolerance. There is no correlation between the enforcement of hate speech laws and the reduction of intolerance. For example, both during the Weimar Republic and in recent decades, Germany has strictly enforced strictly written hate speech laws. Yet Hitler and his Nazi party rose to power during the Weimar period, and the explicitly racist AfD party has grown dramatically in the recent past, with Germany experiencing disturbing upsurges in violence against Jews and other minority groups during both periods.

In the United States, although much progress remains to be made in reducing intolerance, much already has been made since the days of Jim Crow. Yet the Supreme Court did not strongly protect freedom of speech, including for hate speech, until the 1960s. In fact, in 1951, the Court rejected a First Amendment challenge to an Illinois hate speech law, albeit by a deeply divided 5–4 vote. In other words, reduced intolerance in the United States accompanied reduced government power to suppress hate speech, not the opposite. In fact, civil rights leaders and historians concur that robust speech protection, extending even to hate speech, was necessary for promoting the racial justice cause. This book describes many cases that illustrate how local officials routinely wielded any speech-restrictive laws—not to mention many general laws, such as those against breach of the peace and disorderly conduct—to stifle civil rights advocacy. In sum, there is not even a correlation between censoring hate speech and promoting equality, let alone a causal relationship. Censorship of hate speech has accompanied the rise of hatred, and the absence of such censorship has accompanied the rise of equality.

One of the multiple non-censorial strategies to counter hate speech's potential negative impact is counterspeech, in all of its myriad varieties. Multiple reports by human rights activists in many countries and in international agencies have concluded that counterspeech should be prioritized over censorship. Even though these other countries permit non-emergency restrictions on hate speech as consistent with their legal concept of free speech, the human rights experts have concluded that counterspeech is preferable from a pragmatic perspective. For instance, the European Commission against Racism and Intolerance, which monitors the implementation of the many European hate speech laws, recently concluded that, in contrast with such laws, "counterspeech is *much more likely* to be effective" in countering intolerance (emphasis added).

—Pornography?

The etymological origin of the term "pornography" refers to expression about prostitution; more recently, it has denoted sexual expression that is intended to be sexually arousing. Yet the term has acquired a stigmatizing connotation; most people use it to designate whatever sexual expression they find distasteful. Just as we individuals are widely varying in our choices about sexual matters in general, we are equally diverse in our choices about, and responses to, sexual expression. One person's cherished "erotica" is someone else's reviled "hardcore pornography." Quoting the latter term, Supreme Court Justice Potter Stewart illustrated this point when he famously wrote: "I shall not today attempt further to define the kinds of material I understand to be embraced within that shorthand description, and perhaps I could never succeed in intelligibly doing so. But I know it when I see it." Of course, given the wonderful diversity of individuals' perceptions, perspectives, and proclivities, each of us sees a different "it."

The stigmatizing term "pornography" even has been used by movements at the opposite ends of the political spectrum, with diametrically different views about sexual/gender issues, to demonize diametrically different subsets of sexual expression. In the 1980s, the "radical feminist" anti-pornography movement wielded the "pornography" label against sexual expression that it viewed as undermining women's equality and safety. At the very same time, the same term was wielded by the "Meese Pornography Commission," which was spearheaded by then-Attorney General Ed Meese (under President Ronald Reagan) and championed by "the Religious Right." In stark contrast with the anti-porn feminists, however, the Meese Commission targeted sexual expression that it viewed as undermining "traditional family values" and "the traditional nuclear family." If both camps had their way, virtually all sexual expression would be endangered: all such expression that is pro-feminist (and, hence, antithetical to "traditional family values"); and all such expression that is pro–traditional-family-values (and, hence, antithetical to feminist values).

The same wide-ranging attacks on pornography persist to this day, with various advocates seeking the suppression of very different subsets of sexual expression—hence collectively targeting a wide expanse of such expression. From the right end of the political spectrum, the ramped-up attacks on public and school library books, as well as public school curricula, have focused on books by and about LGBTQ+ people. The term "pornography" (as well as "obscenity") has been invoked to assail these books, and some politicians even have advocated prosecuting librarians and others responsible for making the books available. From the left end of the political spectrum, some proponents of the #MeToo movement (which fights sexual assault and harassment) have renewed the 20th-century feminist anti-pornography crusade against a broad array of sexual expression that they view as subverting women's safety or dignity.

The Supreme Court has held that several, relatively narrowly defined subsets of sexual expression are either wholly excluded from First Amendment protection (obscenity and child pornography) or relegated to receiving only reduced First Amendment protection ("patently offensive" or "indecent" speech over the broadcast media, in mandatory high school assemblies, and in adult businesses located near schools and other places where children are likely to be present). In contrast, the vast majority of sexual expression is constitutionally protected both because of the intrinsic importance of/human interest in sexuality, and because of this expression's integral connection to multiple issues of public concern. Therefore, the wide-ranging attacks on "pornography" can be checked on First Amendment grounds.

Notwithstanding free speech concerns, in both the United States and other countries, various officials and activists have continued to wield the "pornography" charge in seeking to suppress a vast array of artistic, cultural, and religious expression—ranging from the Bible (due to passages that have been condemned as misogynistic pornography) to the feminist health classic *Our Bodies, Ourselves*. In 2019, the Russian feminist artist Yulia Tsvetkova was detained, fined, and subjected to a 15-month, closed-door criminal trial on charges of disseminating pornography, with the prosecution seeking a prison sentence of more than 3 years. An outspoken advocate of feminism and LGBTQ+ rights, Tsvetkova had founded an online group called "Vagina Monologues," which posted artwork depicting female bodies in an effort to counter taboos surrounding it. Underscoring the irreducible vagueness and subjectivity of the term/concept of pornography, Tsvetkova's mother made the following, sadly ironic comment to the Associated Press in 2021: "Yulia has always been against pornography . . . Feminists are against pornography because it's exploitation of women's bodies."

Lest anyone think "it can't happen here," the internationally acclaimed play "The Vagina Monologues" by the self-described feminist playwright and women's rights activist "V" (formerly known as Eve Ensler), to which Tsvetkova was paying tribute, also has repeatedly been impugned as pornographic or objectionable on other grounds right here in the United States—by critics on both the left and the right. Following their usual playbooks, left-leaning critics have complained that the play "objectifies" women as sexual objects, whereas right-leaning critics have complained that the play glorifies sexual freedom and pleasure untethered to procreation and "the traditional nuclear family." Most recently, U.S. campus student groups have canceled their previously annual productions of the play, saying that it "excludes the experiences of transgender women who don't have a vagina."

To be sure, there is a crucial distinction between criminal prosecution of sexual expression, as in Russia, and private-sector critiques of and even suppression of that expression, as in the United States. But it is precisely to prevent majoritarian pressures and preferences from fueling government repression that First Amendment law bars government from imposing non-emergency restrictions on sexual expression.

The enforcement pattern of non-emergency restrictions on pornography tracks the general enforcement pattern of all non-emergency restrictions on controversial speech: They disproportionately target expression that is especially important for traditionally disempowered groups, including women, LGBTQ+ people, and advocates of gender equality and reproductive freedom. The above-described experiences with "The Vagina Monologues" and the recent obscenity initiatives are all too typical.

As this book is being finalized, in May 2023, a draconian federal anti-obscenity law, enacted in 1873, is being invoked to curb women's access to mifepristone, which the FDA (Food and Drug Administration) approved in 2000 for use in terminating a pregnancy during its early stages. The "Comstock Act," which was spearheaded by the controversial "anti-vice" crusader Anthony Comstock, outlaws "obscene, lewd, or lascivious" materials, and in the same phrase outlaws "any article. . . intended for the prevention of conception or procuring of abortion," as well as "any . . . information" about any of the prohibited materials—thus expressly conflating expression about contraception and abortion with other expression outlawed as "obscene." In 1914, pioneering birth control advocate Margaret Sanger was indicted under the Comstock Act for giving women information about their reproductive health and options. Now, more than a century later, the Comstock Act's sweeping conception (pun intended) of illegal obscenity has been invoked to curb the distribution of mifepristone. In February 2023, 20 Republican lawmakers cited the Act in letters to CVS and Walgreens pharmacies, threatening them with legal action if they distributed mifepristone. In April 2023, a federal judge in Texas ordered a hold on the FDA's approval of mifepristone, citing the Comstock Act in his opinion.

Even the very type of "feminist anti-pornography" law that some feminists have championed—which outlaws sexual expression that is "degrading" or "dehumanizing" to women—foreseeably has been used disproportionately to stifle expression that is especially important to women and feminists, including even anti-pornography advocacy by the feminist proponents of such laws themselves. In 1992, some Canadian feminists persuaded the Canadian Supreme Court, in a case called *Butler v. The Queen*, to incorporate this concept into Canada's anti-obscenity law. Anti-censorship feminists had long warned that any such legal concept would predictably be used not to advance women's equality or safety, but rather to stifle expression on behalf of disempowered groups, including women and LGBTQ+ people. Alas, those predictions swiftly proved correct. Among the many pertinent books that Canada Customs seized at the United States–Canada border were two anti-pornography books—including *Pornography: Men Possessing Women*—written by one of the two major architects of the (intendedly) feminist anti-pornography approach: Andrea Dworkin. Customs officials explained that these books "illegally eroticized pain and bondage."

Because of this enforcement experience, even the Canadian pro-censorship feminist organization that had championed the *Butler* decision, the Women's Legal Education and Action Fund (LEAF), was quickly forced to acknowledge *Butler*'s pernicious effects on equality goals. LEAF joined with anti-censorship feminists in 1993 to issue a joint news release that "condemned the use of the *Butler* decision to justify the discriminatory use of laws to harass and intimidate lesbians and gays." The LEAF signatories further conceded that "[s]ince . . . *Butler* . . . Canada Customs, some police forces . . . and some government funders have exploited obscenity law to harass bookstores, artists, and AIDS organizations, sex trade workers, and safe sex educators."

In sum, regardless of how pornography is defined, and regardless of the precise goals of those who advocate restricting it, these restrictions inevitably end up targeting much sexual expression about matters of public concern, and much that is highly valued by people across the political spectrum, including anti-pornography activists on both ends of that spectrum.

—Violent speech?

Consistent with the emergency principle, speech may be punished when it has a sufficiently direct connection to violence, and the Supreme Court has recognized several subcategories of such speech that government may punish:

- Intentional incitement of imminent violence, which is likely to happen imminently
- "Fighting words"—direct, face-to-face personal insults, which are intended and likely to produce an immediate violent response
- Solicitation or facilitation of specific violent acts against specific individuals
- "True threats"—speech directly targeting a single individual or small group, when the speaker intends to instill a reasonable fear in listeners that they will be subject to imminent violence.

Additionally, the Court has permitted the indirect sanctioning of violent rhetoric, when such rhetoric constitutes evidence that a victim of criminal violence was intentionally singled out for discriminatory reasons, and therefore subject to increased punishment under "hate crimes" or "bias crimes" laws.

Before the modern Supreme Court adopted the emergency principle, it permitted the government to restrict speech with only a more speculative, attenuated connection to potential violence, thus giving the government essentially unlimited power to punish any speech whose message it disfavored. Unsurprisingly, this discretion was disproportionately exercised to silence speech that criticized government policies and advocated reform. As ACLU Legal Director David Cole observed: "A. Mitchell Palmer, J. Edgar Hoover, and Joseph McCarthy all used the advocacy of violence as a justification to punish people who associated with Communists, socialists, or civil rights groups."

Ironically, during the civil rights movement, even peaceful demonstrators against Jim Crow in the Deep South were criminally convicted for breach of the peace because of the feared violent reactions to their ideas, which local communities and officials viewed as dangerous. Multiple Supreme Court decisions overturned these convictions because the speech did not satisfy the emergency standard; such decisions thus simultaneously advanced free speech and equal rights.

Likewise, in its 1969 *Tinker v. Des Moines* ruling, the Court enforced the emergency principle to protect speech that had been suppressed because of a speculative, "undifferentiated" fear that it might cause violence due to its unpopular message: criticizing the Vietnam War. Consistent with the viewpoint-neutrality principle, the Court explained that the controversial nature of expression constitutes a reason to protect it, not to suppress it. Acknowledging the "discomfort . . . that always accompan[ies] an unpopular viewpoint," and officials' worries that the audience members' negative reactions might lead to violence, the Court nonetheless concluded that "undifferentiated fear or apprehension of" such potential violence "is not enough to overcome the right to freedom of expression." Any contrary holding would become a license to silence dissent—as, indeed, did happen before the Court adopted the emergency principle.

The above-described cases illustrate a point on which the next answer elaborates: It is especially unjust to suppress speech based on a speculative fear that it might lead to violence when the feared violence is anticipated from the speakers' opponents, rather than the speakers' supporters—that is, when speakers intentionally incite their supporters to engage in violence. Even if "hostile audience" members directly threaten imminent violence, such retaliatory anti-speaker violence would justify punishing the threatening hostile audience members, not the speaker.

—Speech that could provoke retaliatory violence against the speaker or others?

Current First Amendment law permits government to restrict speech due to its potential provocation of retaliatory violence against the speaker or others (such as the speaker's supporters or other audience members) in only one strictly limited situation: under the current narrow concept of punishable fighting words. Consistent with the emergency principle, punishable fighting words constitute a type of punishable intentional incitement: a face-to-face insult that the speaker directly hurls at another person, intending to provoke a violent response. The Supreme Court has struck down every one of the multiple fighting words convictions it has reviewed under this standard, because law enforcement officials had invoked the fighting words concept to punish speech that fell far short of it, including much speech that protested the officials' conduct.

The contemporary fighting words doctrine does not justify suppressing speech due to potential retaliatory violence against a speaker or others when the speaker discusses a general idea and addresses a general audience. This important precept is illustrated by *Texas v. Johnson*, the Court's 1989 decision protecting the First Amendment right to burn the American flag in political protest. The government argued that the flag burning at issue angered and offended many onlookers, who therefore might have been provoked to assault the flag burner (no such assault actually occurred). The Court concluded, though, that this expression did not "fall within [the] small class of" punishable fighting words, because "[n]o reasonable onlooker would have regarded" the "generalized expression of dissatisfaction with [government] policies . . . as a direct personal insult or an invitation to exchange fisticuffs."

Modern First Amendment law has rejected the notion that speech may be restricted because of concerns that "hostile audience" members, who reject speakers' views, might threaten or commit violence against speakers or others. In *The Negro and the First Amendment*, his classic 1965 book about the essential role that the Supreme Court's modern speech-protective decisions played in the civil rights movement, University of Chicago Law Professor Harry Kalven coined the term "hecklers' veto" to describe the common pattern before these decisions. When peaceful civil rights demonstrators were greeted by hostile audience members, local officials too often permitted these "hecklers" to "veto" or cancel the free speech rights of speakers and audience members who wanted to hear them. Too often the officials failed to punish the hecklers for threatening and violent conduct, instead suppressing and even punishing the speakers—for example, under laws against breach of the peace or disorderly conduct. In effect, Kalven concluded, the government transferred "the power of censorship to the crowd."

In contrast, the modern Supreme Court has consistently held that it is government's responsibility to protect speakers and audience members from threats and violence, thereby simultaneously protecting their free speech rights. Consequently, the Court repeatedly overturned hecklers' vetoes against pro–civil rights and anti–Vietnam War speakers. Consistent with the general emergency/strict scrutiny standard, the Court has insisted that hostile audience concerns may justify suppressing speech only as a last resort, in situations that should occur extremely rarely, if ever: when government could not protect public safety in any other way.

In the recent past, we have witnessed multiple incidents of government officials, including at public universities, invoking this last-resort rationale for suppressing speech because of concerns about disrupters' violence. An example occurred just a few days before I wrote this passage. At Pennsylvania State University on October 24, 2022, an event hosted by a student organization called "Uncensored America," featuring Proud Boys founder Gavin McInnes, was canceled shortly before it was due to begin. The university's official statement explained: "Due to the threat of escalating violence . . . , Penn State University Police determined that it was necessary to cancel the speaking event in the interest of campus safety." To its credit, the university had resisted pressures to cancel the event shortly after it had been announced, citing free speech principles. However, university officials said that the last-minute reversal was prompted by unidentified "individuals" in the crowd assembled outside the event venue, who "resorted to physical confrontation and to using pepper spray against others in the crowd, including against police officers."

The university president condemned those on both sides who had contributed to the violence, ruing that "the message too many people will walk away with is that one can manipulate people to generate free publicity, or that one can restrict speech by escalating protest to violence," adding that "[t]hese are not ideas that we can endorse as an institution of higher education."

Recent years have witnessed multiple assassinations of people who engaged in expression that the assassins viewed as insulting to Islam; these incidents have sparked the term "assassins' veto." Just as hecklers should not be allowed to temporarily silence speech, it is even more urgent that assassins should not be allowed to permanently silence speakers. If fear of retaliatory violence and murder induces writers, publishers, and others not to engage in targeted expression, then the assassins will have accomplished their purpose. Worse yet, any such coerced self-censorship encourages further threats and violence. As the Free Speech Debates blog commented: "Capitulating to violent intimidation could potentially save lives in the short term, but it could also lead to greater . . . violence if people decide that killing is the most effective way to air their grievances and win their way."

—Extremist or terrorist speech?

As the old saying puts it, "one person's 'terrorist' is another's 'freedom fighter.'" Likewise, one person's "terrorist" or "extremist" speech is another's freedom-fighting advocacy. I will cite just two current illustrations. Influential politicians have denounced Black Lives Matter advocacy as "extremist" or "terrorist" speech (critics also condemn BLM expression with the equally vague epithets "hate speech" and "disinformation"/ "misinformation"). In parallel fashion, in a fall 2021 letter to U.S. Attorney General Merrick Garland, the National School Boards Association denounced parents who were protesting various public school policies, including COVID requirements and the (alleged) teaching of "critical race theory," for engaging in "a form of domestic terrorism."

Multiple answers throughout this book spotlight the integral role that heated rhetoric plays in the vigorous political debates that are so crucial in our democracy. In consequence, it's not surprising that partisans on all sides of multifarious causes brand the speech of their ideological adversaries as "extremist" or even "terrorist." Yet it's one thing for members of our society to accuse each other of engaging in extremist/terrorist expression (such accusations, no matter how baseless, constituted protected speech), but it's another thing entirely for government to be empowered to enforce non-emergency restrictions on such a vague, broad swath of speech, including much speech of public concern.

Whenever anyone has the discretion to enforce such irreducibly subjective restrictions, much valuable speech is inevitably suppressed. Non-emergency restrictions on extremist/terrorist speech would even endanger speech that is antithetical to extremism/terrorism, including human rights advocacy. This counterproductive result is demonstrated by the experience of social media companies, which have come under increasing pressure to restrict extremist/terrorist speech. Even though these tech giants have enormous human and technical resources for identifying the targeted speech, they still have engaged in the unavoidable over-enforcement (as well as under-enforcement) that bedevils such inescapably vague concepts. These problems were detailed in a 2019 joint report by three human rights organizations: Electronic Frontier Foundation, Syrian Archive, and Witness. The report pointed out that both algorithmic and human content-moderation techniques have "caught in the net" "not only content deemed extremist, but also . . . useful content like human rights documentation," with "mistakes at scale that are decimating human rights content." The report elaborated: "[I]t is difficult for human reviewers—and impossible for machines—to consistently differentiate

activism, counterspeech, and satire about extremism from extremism itself. . . . [M]arginalized users are the ones who pay
for [the inevitable] mistakes." In the same vein, a 2017 *New York
Times* story described how YouTube, in its "effort to purge extremist propaganda from its platform," had "inadvertently
removed thousands of videos that could be used to document
atrocities in Syria, potentially jeopardizing future war crimes
prosecutions."

Paralleling the general patterns concerning non-emergency
restrictions on speech with any controversial content, such
restrictions on extremist/terrorist speech do not materially
advance their anti-violence and anti-terrorism goals, but
to the contrary may well undermine these goals. In a comprehensive 2017 report, the Electronic Frontier Foundation
concluded: "[T]he question is not whether terrorists are
using the Internet to recruit new operatives—the question is
whether taking down pro-terrorism content and accounts will
meaningfully contribute to the fight against global terrorism.
Governments have not sufficiently demonstrated this to be
the case. And some experts believe this absolutely not to be
the case."

A non-censorial approach toward extremist/terrorist expression shares a key advantage of a non-censorial approach
toward hate speech: It permits law enforcement and counter-
terrorism officials to monitor individuals who engage in this
expression, for purposes of detecting, deterring, and punishing any planned illegal and violent actions. A 2012 United
Nations (U.N.) report, "The Use of the Internet for Terrorist
Purposes," concluded that "authorities are developing increasingly sophisticated tools to proactively prevent . . . terrorist
activity" detected through extremists' online communications.
Conversely, censorship frustrates counterterrorism efforts,
including intelligence gathering and the amassing of evidence that can be used to prosecute terrorists. The U.N. report observed: "A significant amount of knowledge about the

functioning, activities and sometimes the targets of terrorist organizations is derived from . . . Internet communications. Further, increased Internet use for terrorist purposes provides a corresponding increase in the availability of electronic data which may be compiled and analysed for counter-terrorism purposes."

Another reason why counterterrorism experts conclude that censoring extremist/terrorist content may well be counterproductive also tracks the hate speech situation: Censorship forecloses opportunities for constructive engagement, via counterspeech, that could avert terrorist acts. For example, a Kenyan government official opposed shutting down a Twitter account of the Al Shabaab terrorist organization, because "Al Shabaab needs to be engaged positively and [T]witter is the only avenue."

—Disinformation or misinformation?

Consistent with the emergency principle, the government may punish false speech when it directly, immediately causes specific serious harm. Important examples of punishable false speech include defamation, fraud, and perjury. The term "disinformation" (or "misinformation"[2]) has no specific legal meaning, but is widely used to describe false or misleading speech that cannot constitutionally be punished precisely because its potential harms are diffuse and speculative.

Current debates show that one person's cherished truth is someone else's despised or feared "fake news." Speech that critics seek to suppress as disinformation almost never consists of objectively verifiable/falsifiable facts alone, but rather also involves subjective matters of interpretation and analysis. After all, speakers who intentionally or recklessly utter false factual statements often may be constitutionally punished under existing laws such as those against fraud and defamation. In contrast, though, the Supreme Court has ruled that "[u]nder the First Amendment there is no such thing as a false idea. However pernicious an opinion may seem, we depend for its correction . . . on the competition of other ideas."

If government were permitted to determine which ideas should be punishable as "false," most vulnerable would be ideas that challenge government policy. Until the Supreme Court's historic 1964 *New York Times v. Sullivan* decision, which reined in the concept of punishable defamation, Southern officials systematically pursued multiple defamation lawsuits against civil rights activists and national media outlets for even trivial factual inaccuracies,[3] with the specific goal of stifling both sets of speakers. In the *Sullivan* case alone—which was only one of many such lawsuits that various Southern officials were pursuing—the defendants were facing $500,000 in damages, or about $4.8 million in 2023 dollars. In short, the pre-1964 defamation law, which permitted government to punish disinformation, was weaponized against the government's critics.

To this day, expression by racial justice advocates continues to be assailed as disinformation. For instance, a May 25, 2021, NPR story quoted Mike Gonzalez, a senior fellow with the Heritage Foundation, as stating: "I feel that Black Lives Matter is one of the greatest sources of disinformation. . . . They have manipulated the good nature of many people." To be sure, such charges of disinformation themselves constitute protected speech—indeed, the very type of "counterspeech" that is the appropriate response to any speech that is believed to be false or misleading. My point is that government should not be empowered to deploy this malleable concept as a basis for censorship.

The inherent problems with censoring disinformation in general plague recent laws that are touted as restricting pandemic-related disinformation in particular. *The Economist* reported in February 2021 that "[c]ensorious governments are abusing fake news laws," invoking the pandemic as "an excuse to gag reporters" and to silence critics of their anti-pandemic policies. Given the inescapable elasticity of the concept of disinformation, restrictions on it can easily be wielded against important information, even in democratic countries. Throughout the pandemic, we have witnessed constantly evolving and shifting views among expert individuals and agencies, as they continuously gather and analyze additional data. Yesterday's life-endangering disinformation can—and has—become today's life-protecting gospel. As one example, recall the CDC's (Centers for Disease Control and Prevention's) changing edicts about mask-wearing.

Because of these unavoidable problems with outlawing COVID-related disinformation, in May 2020, the ACLU brought a lawsuit against Puerto Rico's law that made it a crime to knowingly raise a "false alarm" about public emergencies; in March 2020, Puerto Rico's governor had decreed a state of emergency due to the COVID pandemic. The complainants were two prominent investigative journalists, who explained that "developing stories on matters of immense public concern are often complex, contentious, and murky," so that "inadvertent inaccuracies are inevitable even in the most thoroughly vetted reporting." Shortly after the laws went into effect, the Puerto Rican government charged a leading clergyman with allegedly disseminating false information on WhatsApp, about a rumored executive order to close all businesses. In fact, however, only a short time later, the governor did issue just such an order.

In April 2023, the federal judge in the ACLU case struck down Puerto Rico's law, declaring that "[t]he watchdog function of speech is never more vital than during a large-scale crisis." Touting the time-honored counterspeech approach, the judge observed: "[I]nstead of criminalizing speech, the Legislature could simply have required the Government to use its multiple communications platforms to present a complete and accurate description of the facts" about COVID and other emergencies.

The judge's recommended strategy is supported by multiple studies, which have concluded that the most fruitful anti-disinformation tool is accurate information that can check its spread and influence, including proactive dissemination of accurate information; targeted responses to specific disinformation; and preemptive general educational approaches, enhancing information literacy and critical media skills. Psychological research shows that even more effective than debunking disinformation after its distribution is "pre-bunking." A study published in the August 2022 *Science Advances* journal demonstrated the successful impact of this approach on people with various political beliefs, and concerning various conspiracy theories. Its authors analogized pre-bunking to medical immunization: "Pre-emptively warning and exposing people to weakened doses of misinformation can cultivate 'mental antibodies' against fake news." In sum, in contrast with censorship, these "counterspeech"/ "more speech" strategies not only are more compatible with free speech and democracy; they also are more effective in promoting truth.

—Offensive speech?

In two narrow factual contexts, the Supreme Court has upheld government's power to restrict "patently offensive" speech (which is sometimes also referred to as "indecent"): on the over-the-air broadcast media, and in a high school student's speech at a schoolwide assembly that all students were required to attend, including young teenagers. The Court issued these holdings in older decisions (the most recent was issued in 1986) that have been strongly criticized and not recently reexamined.

In all other factual contexts, the Court consistently has struck down government restrictions even on "patently offensive" expression, as well as on the broader category of "offensive" expression. For example, the Court has invalidated government measures that restricted "patently offensive" expression in all other media that it has considered, aside from over-the-air broadcast media.

The Court's refusal to permit non-emergency restrictions on offensive speech has been a consistent hallmark of its rulings, dating all the way back to its unanimous 1940 decision in *Cantwell v. Connecticut*, long before it adopted other speech-protective stances. Even though listeners were "highly offended" by the speech of Jehovah's Witness preacher Jesse Cantwell, which conveyed "a general attack on all organized religious systems as instruments of Satan and injurious to man," and even though the Court found that his expression would "naturally offend" most listeners, it nevertheless spurned those facts as purported justifications for restricting the speech. The Court hailed the vital role that offensive speech plays in our pluralistic democracy:

> In the realm of religious faith, and in that of political belief, sharp differences arise. . . . [T]he tenets of one man may seem the rankest error to his neighbor. To persuade others to his own point of view, the pleader at times resorts to exaggeration, to vilification . . . , and even to false statement. But the people of this nation have ordained . . . that . . . these liberties are, in the long view, essential to enlightened opinion . . . on the part of the citizens of a democracy.

Cantwell further recognized that protection for offensive speech is especially "necessary . . . in our . . . country, for a people composed of many races and of many creeds." In short, the First Amendment's protection of offensive speech reflects its equal protection of diverse identities and beliefs.

Whether a particular expression or idea is "offensive" is an irreducibly subjective matter, turning on the perceptions and beliefs of each individual audience member, not to mention countless contextual factors that affect the overall message, beyond the words themselves—for instance, a speaker's tone of voice and accompanying facial expressions and gestures. The

Supreme Court acknowledged this problem with punishing offensive speech in its 1971 *Cohen v. California* ruling, which upheld the right to wear a jacket proclaiming "Fuck the draft" at a time when that phrase was doubly offensive to many people. First, the anti-draft opinion was highly offensive to the many people who viewed it as undermining national security and insulting toward military personnel, including those who had been killed or injured in the war, and their family members. Second, the word that conveyed this opinion was also highly offensive—so much so that Supreme Court Chief Justice Warren Burger refused to utter it, and also implored the Justice who authored the Court's opinion (John Marshall Harlan II) not to include it in the opinion.

The *Cohen* decision memorably captured the inescapably subjective nature of "offensiveness," observing that "one [person]'s vulgarity is another's lyric." Therefore, if government had power to restrict speech that anyone—even many people—considered offensive, there would be hardly any speech left. Just consider the wide, divergent array of expression that has been attacked as offensive, including artistic, political, and religious expression that many people consider highly valuable. As the *Cohen* Court concluded: "[I]t is largely because governmental officials cannot make principled distinctions in this area that the Constitution leaves matters of taste and style so largely to the individual."

The *Cohen* Court rejected the suggestion that government could "simply" require Paul Cohen to reframe his message by omitting the particular epithet that others considered offensive, without suppressing the message itself: "[W]e cannot indulge the facile assumption that one can forbid particular words without also running a substantial risk of suppressing ideas in the process. Indeed, governments might soon seize upon the censorship of particular words as a convenient guise for banning the expression of unpopular views." This was the overt goal of the "Newspeak" language in George Orwell's

1984, which deliberately banned certain words in order to banish the "subversive" ideas they conveyed.[4]

The *Cohen* case illustrates a significant shared pattern among non-emergency restrictions on offensive speech, which traces all the way back to the 1940 *Cantwell* case: The expression typically involves unpopular, dissenting perspectives regarding matters of public concern. Expression that critiques—or even just questions—prevailing political, cultural, or religious values in a particular community is frequently attacked as "offensive." In his memoir, author Salman Rushdie uses the label "thought crimes" to link together the many cases, beyond his own, in which "writers and intellectuals across the Islamic world [have been] accused" of "blasphemy, heresy, apostasy, insult, and offense." Given the malleability of the epithet "offensive"—as well as all these related terms—permitting speech restrictions on any such rationale would, Rushdie concludes, serve "the accusers' real project: the stifling of heterodoxy and dissent."

—Incivility?

It is certainly appropriate for public (as well as private) institutions, such as universities, to encourage members of their communities to express themselves in a civil and respectful manner. For instance, such encouragement was incorporated in the "Chicago Free Speech Principles," which the University of Chicago adopted in 2014, and which since have been adopted by many diverse public and private higher education institutions all over the United States. The pertinent language states: "Although the University greatly values civility, and although all members of the University community share in the responsibility for maintaining a climate of mutual respect, concerns about civility and mutual respect can never be used as a justification for closing off discussion of ideas, however offensive or disagreeable those ideas may be to some members of our community."

Such an encouragement of civility embodies two important limits. First, the institution encourages a particular *manner* of expressing ideas, with no limit at all on *which* ideas are expressed. All things being equal, if we can convey our viewpoints through words, tones, gestures, and facial expressions that signal civility and respect, we should be encouraged to do so, and we should do so voluntarily. However, if a particular viewpoint could not be conveyed through words and other means that audience members are likely to regard as civil and respectful, we should nonetheless convey it.

Second, university and other public officials may not enforce any general civility requirement. Accordingly, if an individual deliberately chooses to convey a message in an uncivil—even disrespectful—manner, that individual choice must be protected. Indeed, the incivility and disrespect may very well constitute integral elements of the substantive message. Consider, for example, messages that protest certain official conduct. If a member of the community objects to police misconduct, she may convey her disrespect for the conduct, and for the officers who engaged in it, through intentionally disrespectful language. Other answers throughout this book cite specific examples of such language targeting police officers and other officials.

In the preceding paragraph, I deliberately indicated that university officials may not enforce any "general" civility requirement because of the following caveat: Faculty members at public higher education institutions could certainly choose to enforce specific civility requirements for their class discussions, as a viewpoint-neutral "manner" restriction on speech, to promote important pedagogical and professional training goals. For example, in my law school classes, I have required all students to convey all of their viewpoints in appropriately "professional" and "lawyerly" language, which would be suitable for a court of law or other legal setting.

The Supreme Court has repeatedly recognized that, especially in debates about public affairs, participants are likely to communicate in ways that are far from civil, and that such communications are essential for both democratic discourse and individual liberty. In today's contentious campus climate, many student activists have communicated their objections to ideas of invited speakers, and to actions of university officials, as well as other students, in language that is harsh and insulting in both content and the manner of delivery. Multiple widely circulated videotapes show students boisterously, rudely interrupting attempted statements by speakers and university officials by shouting out insults, including vulgar epithets. For example, in the fall of 2015, Yale undergraduates angrily surrounded and shouted at Professor Nicholas Christakis, in his capacity as "faculty-in-residence" of one of Yale's residential colleges, because they rejected his view that the college should be a forum for exchanging ideas, not solely a place of "comfort" analogous to a home. One student screamed at him: "Who the fuck hired you?! You should step down! . . . You should not sleep at night! You are disgusting!" Could these students effectively convey their strongly held views and impassioned emotional reactions through language that is constrained to be civil in content or manner of delivery?[5]

Reflecting a major general problem with all non-emergency speech restrictions, the "uncivil" speech that the Supreme Court has protected against government suppression, unsurprisingly, has often conveyed criticism of government officials and policies; recall, for example, Paul Cohen's jacket proclaiming "Fuck the Draft." In today's context, any civility code would no doubt be enforced against people who are protesting current government policies and actions, ranging from police practices to pandemic measures. Similarly, campus officials would likely enforce such codes against critics of their policies. On all sides of controversial issues, individuals with strong views are unlikely to confine their communications to those that other people, including officials, consider civil—nor should they be required to do so.

—Blasphemy?

"Blasphemy" is the stigmatizing term for expression that challenges a prevailing religious orthodoxy. Any non-emergency restriction on blasphemy would blatantly violate the core viewpoint-neutrality principle. Any such restriction would also blatantly violate the parallel neutrality principle that undergirds the First Amendment's religious liberty guarantees: that government may neither favor nor disfavor any religious belief. In both contexts, the unifying notion is that ideas and beliefs are for individuals to formulate and espouse, exercising their freedom of conscience without government coercion or interference. This fundamental notion was eloquently enshrined in the 1943 flag salute decision, decreeing that government may not "prescribe what shall be orthodox in politics, nationalism, religion, or other matters of opinion."

Not only are restrictions on blasphemy antithetical to individual freedom; they are also antithetical to democracy and the search for truth. As the playwright George Bernard Shaw observed, "All great truths begin as blasphemies." His observation applies to all spheres of human endeavor, including government and natural science. In a democracy, where "We the People" wield sovereign political power, we must be free to air and discuss all perspectives on matters of public concern—even perspectives that some religions consider blasphemous. Many religions propound doctrines about matters of public concern, including abortion, LGBTQ+ rights, and vaccinations, to cite several current examples. If members of the public and government officials were barred from advocating policies on such matters because these policies were inconsistent with some religious dogma, we would be living in a theocracy, not a democracy.

Along with other non-emergency speech restrictions, blasphemy laws are disproportionately enforced to silence dissent and persecute minorities. In Pakistan, for instance, blasphemy laws are regularly enforced against members of the Hindu minority. In a shocking recent example, in 2021 an 8-year-old Hindu boy was charged with blasphemy—a capital offense—because he urinated on a carpet in the library of a madrassa (a college for Islamic instruction). Even in modern democratic countries, various laws, including those targeting hate speech, have functioned as anti-blasphemy laws, because they are used to punish expression that is deemed insulting to religious beliefs. For example, Italian comedian Sabina Guzzanti was subject to criminal investigation in 2008, facing a potential 5-year prison sentence, for joking at a rally that Pope Benedict XVI would go to hell and be tormented by gay demons. And Britain joined Pakistan in subjecting a minor to such laws; in 2008, a 15-year-old British boy was criminally charged and investigated for participating in a demonstration while holding a sign with this message: "Scientology is not a religion, it is a dangerous cult."

In recent years, the following argument has been raised to support banning certain allegedly blasphemous speech: that it is likely to trigger a violent response by offended religious believers. This argument arose, for instance, in the aftermath of "the Danish cartoons controversy": the 2005 publication of cartoons depicting the prophet Muhammad, which was followed by violent riots and associated deaths in several Muslim countries. In 2012, the United States was pressured to censor an online video that was widely criticized as anti-Islamic and was blamed (wrongly, as it later turned out) for having spurred the murderous attack on the U.S. Embassy in Benghazi, Libya. In a speech to the UN General Assembly shortly after this terrorist attack, President Barack Obama laid out not only the principled reasons why the expression at issue should not be censored, but also the practical, strategic reasons why such censorship would undermine its goal of preventing violence: "There are no words that excuse the killing of inno-cents. . . . In this modern world with modern technologies, for us to respond in [a censorial] way to hateful speech empowers any individual who engages in such speech to create chaos around the world. We empower the worst of us if that's how we respond."

A 2017 petition to the Danish Parliament, calling for the repeal of Denmark's blasphemy law—which was subse-quently repealed—well summarized the wrongheadedness of suppressing blasphemy for the purpose of preventing respon-sive violence by those who object to it: "In a liberal democracy, laws protect those who offend from threats, not those who threaten from being offended." Readers will recognize that this is precisely the approach that the modern Supreme Court has adopted; it has consistently held that "hostile audience" members may not wield a "hecklers' veto"—or, worse yet, an "assassins' veto"—against expression they reject.

—Speech that causes emotional distress?

... when the speech is about matters of public concern?

Since the late 19th century, American courts have recognized that certain conduct, including expressive conduct, could con-stitute the tort of "intentional infliction of emotional distress" (IIED), for which victims could seek damages in civil lawsuits. Consistent with the free speech concerns at stake, courts have narrowly circumscribed the situations in which such a tort ac-tion would arise, requiring the actionable conduct to be "out-rageous" and the ensuing distress to be "severe." [6]

Moreover, the Supreme Court has imposed additional First Amendment limits on IIED claims that are based on expres-sion. The Court has decided two cases on point, in both of which it held that the speech at issue addressed matters of public concern, which is of utmost importance in our demo-cratic republic, and hence may not be suppressed through tort lawsuits any more than through the criminal law.

In these two cases, the Court did not completely foreclose IIED lawsuits arising from speech, but it did essentially foreclose such lawsuits when the speech primarily addresses matters of public concern. Moreover, the Court has broadly defined the public concern concept as "relating to any matter of political, social, or other concern to the community." In its 2011 ruling in *Snyder v. Phelps*, the Court overturned an IIED damages award to the father of Marine Lance Corporal Matthew Snyder, who had been killed in the line of duty in Iraq. The award had been based on signs that picketers carried near Matthew Snyder's funeral, conveying hateful, insulting messages about the U.S. military, the Catholic Church, and LGBTQ+ people. Although some of the hateful messages specifically targeted Matthew Snyder and his family, the Court determined that "the overall thrust and dominant theme" of the picketing "spoke to broader public issues."

Hate speech and other controversial expression that could well cause emotional distress for particular audience members—including blasphemy and rhetoric that is offensive, uncivil, or violent—generally addresses public issues, as the Supreme Court broadly defines such issues. Just consider some previously referenced examples of expression that government has sought to restrict on the rationale that it constituted one of these types of controversial speech, but that the Supreme Court protected: a neo-Nazi demonstration in a community that was home to many Holocaust survivors and other Jewish people; burning the U.S. flag in political protest; wearing a jacket with the message "Fuck the Draft"; wearing a black armband to protest the Vietnam War; and making threatening statements against people who patronized businesses that engaged in racial discrimination. In most of these cases, the government expressly argued that it should have power to restrict the speech because of the speech's upsetting impact on audience members—the very same harm that underlies the IIED tort action. Indeed, if emotional distress could justify restricting speech, one is hard pressed to think of any government official, political candidate, or individual activist who would not be subject to censorship, given the "vituperative" and "abusive" language that, as the Supreme Court observed, is "often" "used in the political arena."

In barring IIED recoveries for controversial speech addressing matters of public concern, the Court has not at all minimized the significant psychological and even physiological harm that such speech can inflict. To the contrary, the *Snyder* opinion cited the expert witness testimony that "the emotional anguish" of the plaintiff, Matthew Snyder's father, "had resulted in severe depression and had exacerbated pre-existing health conditions." Nonetheless, the Court held that since such distress "turned on the . . . viewpoint of the message conveyed . . . at a public place on a matter of public concern," the "speech is entitled to special protection under the First Amendment." Reiterating a common theme among cases concerning all kinds of controversial speech, the Court concluded that vesting the government with the power to suppress this speech would do more harm than the speech itself.

In both of its IIED cases, the Court underscored the major reason why the harmful potential of controversial speech is less than that of government power to censor it: The targeted speech is inevitably elastic in scope and accordingly is proscribed in unduly vague terms, which the government could wield against disfavored ideas. As the Court observed, the concept of "outrageousness," which is central to the IIED tort, "is a highly malleable standard with an inherent subjectiveness about it which would allow a jury to impose liability. . . on the basis of their dislike of a particular expression."

Given the fluidity and subjectivity of the emotional distress concept, it could be enforced against an extremely broad, diverse range of expression—even speech with diametrically opposing messages. For example, the leading antebellum pro-slavery advocate Senator John C. Calhoun argued that abolitionists who criticized slavery "inflicted emotional injury" on white people in the South. Surely his very own pro-slavery advocacy inflicted emotional injury on countless others. More recently, a 1965 Supreme Court decision upheld the free speech rights of the Reverend Elton B. Cox, a Black minister who had led a civil rights demonstration by Louisiana students, and whose speech had been criminally punished due to the "emotional upset [that] was caused by Cox's remarks about 'black and white together.' "

... even if the speech is not about a matter of public concern?

Even if speech addresses only matters of private concern, non-emergency speech restrictions should still not be based on speech's emotionally distressing impact. The speech-suppressive costs of permitting non-emergency restrictions on any speech that causes emotional distress—even speech that does not pertain to matters of public concern—flows from the difficulty of demonstrating, with objective evidence, any causal connection between speech and psychic harm. Social scientists who specialize in communications have recognized that there has been little empirical investigation of this complex issue, which would be difficult to undertake, given the countless factors that affect how each of us reacts to speech, including who the speaker is and myriad contextual factors surrounding the words themselves.

This point was acknowledged even in law professor Richard Delgado's pathbreaking 1982 article advocating a new tort action for "racial insults" that cause emotional distress. Delgado recognized that "the emotional damage caused" by such insults "is variable and depends on many factors, only one of which is the outrageousness of the insult." Therefore, Delgado acknowledged, even such a loathsome epithet as "nigger [sic]" should not always be actionable; that "[depends] on the speaker's intent, the hearer's understanding, and whether a reasonable person would consider it a racial insult in the particular context."

A previous answer explained why the First Amendment bars non-emergency restrictions on offensive speech. Yet it is difficult to distinguish between speech that assertedly causes emotional distress from offensive speech. This point was a factor in the famous 1977–78 "Skokie case," in which multiple state and federal courts (including the U.S. Supreme Court) upheld the free speech rights of neo-Nazis to demonstrate in Skokie, Illinois, which had a large Jewish population, including many Holocaust survivors. Skokie officials sought to impose non-emergency restrictions on the neo-Nazis' expression on the ground that it might cause "psychological trauma" to Skokie residents. As one court pointed out, though, it is "difficult to distinguish a person who suffers actual psychological trauma from one who is only highly offended, and . . . speech may not be punished merely because it offends."

—Defamation against public officials and figures?

In its landmark 1964 *New York Times v. Sullivan* decision, the Court for the first time applied First Amendment standards to state defamation law, which governs false statements that injure someone's reputation, causing demonstrable financial or other harm. The Court recognized that civil damages actions for the defamation tort could well have punitive and deterrent impacts on speech that equal, or even exceed, the speech-suppressive impacts of criminal prosecutions. For instance, in *Sullivan* itself, the damages that had been imposed ($500,000)[7] were 1,000 times greater than the maximum fine that could have been levied in a criminal libel prosecution ($500).

The defamation lawsuit in the *Sullivan* case had been brought by an Alabama official against civil rights leaders, as well as the *New York Times*, based on an advertisement the civil rights leaders had placed in the *Times*, describing Southern officials' suppression of their rights and seeking financial contributions to their movement. This lawsuit was part of a broad strategy, involving many similar defamation lawsuits, which Southern officials employed in an effort to silence both the civil rights movement and the national media that spread the movement's message. Pre-*Sullivan* state defamation tort law involved essentially "strict" or automatic liability; it permitted massive actual and punitive damages awards to be imposed even for trivial inaccuracies, and even when the speakers and publishers had exercised due care. Consequently, this law could easily be harnessed to silence the media and the civil rights organizations one way or the other: by bankrupting them, or by pressuring them to cease their civil rights advocacy in order to avoid bankruptcy.

Sullivan illustrates two major recurring themes in modern First Amendment law: the special importance of speech about public officials, including critical speech; and the necessity for "prophylactic" rules, which protect even some problematic speech—in this case, some defamatory speech—in order to avoid chilling even nonproblematic, valuable speech. On the first theme, the Court issued one of its most-often-quoted pronouncements, celebrating the "profound national commitment to the principle that debate on public issues should be uninhibited, robust, and wide-open, and that it may well include vehement, caustic, and sometimes unpleasantly sharp attacks on government and public officials." On the second theme, the Court voiced concern that the state tort law may well deter "would-be critics of official conduct . . . from voicing their criticism, even though it is believed to be true and even though it is, in fact, true, because of doubt whether it can be proved in court or fear of the expense of having to do so," thereby "dampen[ing] the vigor . . . of public debate."

Sullivan formulated a special prophylactic rule for defamation actions brought by public officials, which it later extended to defamation actions brought by "public figures"—people who either have celebrity status in general, or who have "thrust themselves into the public spotlight" for purposes of affecting a specific public controversy. To prevail in defamation claims, public officials/figures must prove that the defendants acted either knowingly or recklessly regarding the falsity of the defamatory statements; it would not be enough to show (as it would be in defamation lawsuits brought by non-public officials/figures) that a defendant had acted negligently.[8] Moreover, public official/figure defamation plaintiffs have to make this showing by "clear and convincing evidence," a more demanding evidentiary standard than the usual "preponderance of the evidence" standard in most civil litigation.

6

FIRST AMENDMENT RIGHTS IN SPECIFIC GOVERNMENT INSTITUTIONS

How is First Amendment analysis affected when the government is operating public institutions with specific purposes?

So far, this book has discussed the free speech rights of members of the general public to be protected from unjustified speech restrictions in the general public sphere. Beyond government's general regulatory role, though, it also operates some important institutions with specific public-serving functions: educational institutions, prisons, military facilities, and numerous workplaces. In stark contrast with government-run public parks, which have traditionally served a prime function as "traditional public forums" open to the general public for expressive purposes, these other, special-purpose government-run institutions have other primary purposes. The freewheeling public free speech rights that are protected in traditional public forums would be incompatible with the primary purposes of these other types of government property, which is why the public does not have open access to them for expressive purposes. Likewise, the specific primary purposes of these special-purpose government institutions would also be undermined if the people who are participating in them— students, faculty members, prisoners, military personnel, and employees—had the same freewheeling free speech rights in these settings as they would enjoy as members of the general public in a traditional public forum. Nonetheless, the Supreme Court has held that participants in these settings do have some First Amendment rights, and it has laid out the scope of such rights through its customary case-by-case approach, taking into account the differing expressive concerns and countervailing interests in each type of government institution.

I will summarize the rulings about these various special-purpose government institutions in roughly descending order, from those where the Court has recognized the most First Amendment rights, to those where it has recognized the fewest.

What are students' First Amendment rights in public higher education institutions?

The Supreme Court has recognized an implicit First Amendment right of academic freedom, which accords special autonomy to higher education institutions, and reinforces the free speech rights of faculty members and students. The Court has strongly protected the First Amendment rights of college and university students on campus, treating such rights as essentially identical to those of the general public in the general public sphere. In a 1972 case, the Court decreed: "[S]tate colleges and universities are not enclaves immune from . . . the First Amendment."

Applying the general First Amendment doctrines about various kinds of public property to the campus context, certain areas of campus, such as malls, are treated as traditional public forums, which are open for expressive activities. Likewise, other areas of campus are analogous to limited public forums (which government may make available for speech by certain members of the public and/or about certain topics) and nonpublic forums (which are off-limits for expression by members of the public). For example, university libraries, along with public libraries, may choose to open their meeting rooms during non-business hours to particular speakers (such as students) and/or particular topics (such as course-related topics) on a viewpoint-neutral basis. Nonpublic forums would include areas of the campus whose primary purpose is incompatible with general expressive activities (e.g., science laboratories).

Transposing to the public campus context the viewpoint-neutrality and emergency principles that govern the public sphere at large, the Supreme Court has struck down several campus speech restrictions, including the denial of recognition to a student organization that was controversial on its campus at the time (Students for a Democratic Society [SDS]), and the suppression of an "underground" newspaper, containing expression that many observers considered offensive, pornographic, defamatory, and violent.

I will illustrate the Court's speech-protective stance toward college students by providing some more details about the latter case: the Court's 1973 ruling in *Papish v. Board of Curators*. *Papish* overturned the University of Missouri's expulsion of a journalism student for distributing the *Free Press Underground* on campus, because the University considered two items in this newspaper "indecent": a political cartoon depicting policemen raping the Statue of Liberty and the Goddess of Justice, and an article entitled "M___f__ Acquitted," which addressed the acquittal on an assault charge of a member of an organization known as "Up Against the Wall, M___f___." Notably, the "F-bomb" was considered so toxic and taboo a term at that time that Supreme Court Chief Justice Warren Burger had tried to block its usage even in the oral argument and decision in a case squarely addressing whether its public use could be punished. The federal trial judge in the *Papish* case held that the expression at issue constituted constitutionally unprotected obscenity, and indicated that he might well also consider it constitutionally unprotected fighting words, stating: "The plaintiff . . . intentionally . . . [distributed] the publication to provoke a confrontation with the authorities by pandering the publication with crude, puerile, vulgar obscenities." In overturning the lower court's ruling, the Supreme Court cited decisions it had issued protecting offensive, controversial speech in the general public sphere, and narrowly construing the concepts of constitutionally unprotected obscenity and fighting words, thus underscoring that these decisions applied fully to student speech on public campuses.

What are faculty members' First Amendment rights in public higher education institutions?

The Court has provided some protection to government employees' freedom of speech. These rulings about the general free speech rights of all government employees afford the baseline protection for faculty members at public higher education institutions: In a nutshell, when any public employees speak as "citizens" (the term the Supreme Court uses to indicate that they are not speaking specifically in their employment capacity) on matters of public concern, "they may face only those speech restrictions that are necessary for their employers to operate efficiently and effectively."

Furthermore, the Court has recognized academic freedom as an implicit First Amendment right. Although its academic freedom rulings are few in number and vague in content, they indicate that faculty members at public higher education institutions enjoy some additional speech protections, beyond those of other government employees.

The Court has discussed the scope of faculty members' free speech and academic freedom rights in only a few cases. The Court invoked academic freedom in striking down two McCarthy-era programs: a state legislative investigation into lectures delivered at a state university, and a state loyalty oath program, requiring faculty members to disavow Communist Party membership. More recently, in a 2006 case in which the Court ruled that government employees' First Amendment rights do not protect expression within the scope of their employment duties, it expressly declined to extend that speech-restrictive holding to faculty members at public educational institutions. Instead, alluding to academic freedom, the Court recognized that "expression related to academic scholarship or classroom instruction implicates additional constitutional interests that are not fully accounted for by this Court's customary employee-speech jurisprudence."

Given the paucity of pertinent Supreme Court rulings, the scope of faculty members' free speech/academic freedom in particular factual situations largely has been spelled out through policies adopted by the American Association of University Professors (AAUP) and lower-court decisions. Of particular interest, the AAUP has laid out in the faculty context the general First Amendment protection for all government employees speaking in their role as citizens on matters of public concern. It has said that when faculty members "speak or write as citizens"—that is, when they are not carrying out their professional scholarly and teaching duties—"they should be free from institutional censorship or discipline." The AAUP has elaborated that such "extramural utterances" may be grounds for discipline only when they "raise grave doubts concerning the [faculty member's] fitness for his or her position." Likewise, the AAUP has said, "The controlling principle is that a faculty member's expression of opinion as a citizen cannot constitute grounds for dismissal unless it clearly demonstrates . . . unfitness," adding that "[e]xtramural utterances rarely bear upon . . . fitness" and that "a final decision should take into account the faculty member's entire record as a teacher and scholar."

What are students' First Amendment rights in public schools (K–12)?

Even the pre-modern Supreme Court recognized some significant First Amendment rights on the part of public school students. For example, in its 1943 *West Virginia Board of Education v. Barnette* ruling, which struck down state statutes that required all public school students to salute the American flag, the Court did not intimate that students had fewer First Amendment rights than members of the general public. To the contrary, the Court stressed the special importance of public school students' free speech rights, given the schools' special mission to prepare our nation's young people to exercise their civic responsibilities. Although the Court recognized the "highly discretionary" power that local school boards exercise, the Court also cautioned:

> That they are educating the young for citizenship is reason for scrupulous protection of Constitutional freedoms of the individual, if we are not to strangle the free mind at its source and teach youth to discount important principles of our government as mere platitudes.

In another landmark student free speech case, its 1969 *Tinker v. Des Moines* decision, the Court laid out the current general standard for evaluating students' First Amendment rights, which is consistent with its modern free speech tenets generally. Declaring that "neither students nor teachers shed their Constitutional rights at the schoolhouse gate," *Tinker* bars schools from enforcing any viewpoint-discriminatory rules, and requires schools to validate any speech restriction by showing that it is necessary to prevent a "material" or "substantial" "disruption of the educational process" or a violation of others' rights. This standard transposes to the school context the emergency/strict scrutiny standards for evaluating content-based speech restrictions in the general public sphere. Consistent with the emergency principle, the Court stressed that mere generalized fear or speculation that speech might lead to negative consequences does not warrant restricting it. As the Court recognized, all speech may have a negative impact, which is precisely why this potential impact cannot justify speech restrictions:

[U]ndifferentiated fear or apprehension of disturbance is not enough to overcome the right to freedom of expression. . . . Any variation from the majority's opinion may inspire fear. Any word spoken . . . that deviates from the views of another person may start an argument or cause a disturbance. But our Constitution says we must take this risk; and our history says that it is this sort of hazardous freedom—this kind of openness—that is the basis of our national strength and of the independence and vigor of Americans.

In three student speech cases after its 1969 *Tinker* decision, the Court upheld the specific restrictions on the student speech at issue, focusing on the particular facts in each case that, it concluded, vindicated such restrictions. For instance, in a 1986 case, the Court held that the pertinent speech — student-authored articles in a school newspaper—could fairly be viewed as bearing the school's imprimatur, rather than conveying the students' own views; in that situation, the Court concluded, the school could impose regulations that are "reasonably related to legitimate pedagogical concerns." In a different factual situation, however—for example, if a school newspaper was clearly designated as an independent student publication, expressing students' views, and disclaiming school sponsorship—the *Tinker* standard would apply.

In its most recent student speech case, its 2021 *B.L. v. Mahanoy* ruling, the Court held that a public school could not discipline a student for social media posts made on the student's own mobile phone, sent only to a group of the student's friends, from an off-school location, during non-school time. Although the student's message contained profane language about the school and some of its staff members, and although this message provoked discussion among members of the school community, the Court rejected the school's argument that these factors legitimized the school's punishment of the speech. It stressed the special importance of enforcing general speech-protective principles in the school context, explaining that the interest in "protecting a student's unpopular expression" is shared by both the student and "the school itself," because "America's public schools are the nurseries of democracy," which "only works if we protect the marketplace of ideas."

What are faculty members' First Amendment rights in public schools (K–12)?

Since public school teachers are government employees, their free speech rights are essentially the same as those of other government employees: If the speech is not within the employee's work duties and is about matters of public concern, a court will protect the speech if it determines that, on balance, the public interest in the expression outweighs the employer's interest in an efficient workplace.

There is one respect in which public school teachers' free speech rights might exceed those of other employees. It arises from the Court's 2006 decision holding that the First Amendment does not protect a public employee's freedom of speech regarding any speech that is within the scope of the employee's job duties. The Court stated that this holding might not apply to "expression related to academic scholarship or classroom instruction." While this qualifying language clearly encompasses expression by college/university faculty members, it is not clear whether this language also applies to K–12 teachers.

In a series of cases dating back to 1952, even before the Court significantly protected free speech in general, it "unequivocally rejected" the view that "teachers may constitutionally be compelled to relinquish the First Amendment rights they would otherwise enjoy as citizens to comment on matters of public interest in connection with the operation of the public schools in which they work." To the contrary, the Court has stressed that protecting such expression reinforces the public's right to receive information, as well as securing the teachers' rights to convey it. Likewise, even during the Cold War, the Court held that the First Amendment protected schoolteachers against mandatory loyalty oaths and requirements that they disclose their organizational memberships, parallel to its rulings concerning college/university professors.

More recently, the Court has upheld public school teachers' free speech rights in two cases pursuant to its general balancing test for evaluating whether public employees have free speech rights when addressing matters of public concern. In both cases, the teachers did discuss matters of public concern, and the Court held that the public interest in their speech outweighed the school employers' countervailing interests. In one decision, the Court protected a teacher's right to publish a letter to the editor of a local newspaper, which criticized the school board's allocation of funds. In the second case, decided in 1979, the Court protected a teacher's right to complain to her principal about racial discrimination in her school system. Bessie Burnham Givhan, a Black public school teacher, taught in a Mississippi junior high school that had been integrated in the 1970–71 school year. She complained to her principal that the school with more Black students was not receiving adequate school supplies compared to the schools with more white students. After Ms. Givhan's contract was not renewed, she filed a discrimination lawsuit, and the trial judge concluded that the non-renewal was in retaliation for these critical comments. In a holding that benefited public employees generally, the Supreme Court unanimously rejected "the conclusion that a public employee forfeits" free speech protection for expression about matters of public concern when the employee "decides to express [these] views privately" (i.e., in a private conversation) "rather than publicly."

What are First Amendment rights regarding school curricula and library books?

The Supreme Court has decided only one case about the First Amendment rights implicated by public officials' decisions concerning school curricula and library books. The Court's 1982 ruling in *Island Trees School District v. Pico* was strictly confined to the particular factual issue in that case: a school board's removal of certain books from the school library in response to complaints by a group of parents. The Court stressed that it was not addressing other related but distinguishable decisions by school officials, which might entail different First Amendment analyses: decisions about acquiring library books and decisions about school curricula. *Pico* even acknowledged that school authorities "might well defend their claim of absolute discretion in matters of curriculum by reliance upon their duty to inculcate community values." Further limiting *Pico*'s precedential force is the fact that the Court did not issue a majority opinion, but rather only a plurality opinion. While some federal appellate courts have construed the plurality opinion as a binding precedent expressing the Court's view, other federal appellate courts have reached the contrary conclusion. Nonetheless, since *Pico* is the Court's only case addressing this "largely uncharted field" (to quote a concurring opinion in the case), it merits a summary, given the many recent controversies about school library books and curricula.

The *Pico* plurality opinion recognized the discretionary nature of decisions concerning what topics and books to include in school curricula, and what books to include in school libraries. It also recognized that these discretionary determinations presumptively rest within the control of publicly accountable officials, including school boards, consistent with basic tenets of representative democracy. However, the plurality opinion also held, consistent with previous Court decisions about public schools, that when First Amendment rights are "directly and sharply implicated" by school officials' determinations, courts should "intervene." Moreover, the plurality concluded that students' First Amendment rights may well be "directly and sharply implicated by the removal of books from . . . a school library."

In accordance with the fundamental viewpoint- and speaker-neutrality principles, the *Pico* plurality reasoned that if books are removed from a school library due to viewpoint-neutral concerns such as educational suitability and age-appropriateness, that raises no First Amendment problems. In contrast, if books are removed due to discrimination against either their ideas or their authors, that would violate the First Amendment. In summarizing its holding, the plurality quoted a core phrase from its landmark 1943 flag salute decision, which also arose in the public school context: "[S]chool boards may not remove books from school library shelves simply because they dislike the ideas contained in those books and seek by their removal to 'prescribe what shall be orthodox in politics, nationalism, religion, or other matters of opinion.'"

The *Pico* plurality opinion was supported by four Justices; three of them joined one opinion, with the fourth authoring a separate, concurring opinion, although stating that he agreed with the plurality opinion's legal standard. Four dissenting Justices expressly rejected the plurality's analysis, opining that school authorities' discretion to remove library books would be violated only in the limited situations when the removal reflected "narrowly partisan" or racially discriminatory motives—for example, "[i]f a Democratic school board . . . ordered the removal of all books written by or in favor of Republicans, or if an all-white school board . . . remove[d] all books authored by blacks or advocating racial equality and integration." The ninth Justice, Byron White, expressly declined to opine on the "difficult First Amendment issues" that the case posed "in a largely uncharted field." Since the Court has not returned to this field in the intervening 41 years, it remains "largely uncharted."

What First Amendment rights do government employees have?

Along with private sector employers, when government acts in its capacity as an employer, its primary purpose—and its primary responsibility to the public—is to facilitate the efficient functioning of the workplace. The pre-modern Supreme Court did not recognize any workplace free speech rights for government employees. This position was well captured in an often-quoted judicial opinion by Oliver Wendell Holmes, before he joined the U.S. Supreme Court. Although Holmes was then a Justice on Massachusetts's highest court, his statement reflected the nationwide law on this issue until 1968. Rejecting the free speech claim of a Boston police officer who had been fired for expressing political views, Holmes wrote: "[He] may have a constitutional right to talk politics, but he has no constitutional right to be a policeman."

Consistent with the modern Court's general expansion of free speech rights across many specific doctrinal areas, it has rejected Holmes's reasoning and recognized that people should not have to forfeit First Amendment rights as the price of government employment. Further, the Court has recognized the public interest in receiving information and ideas from government employees, who may well have special insights into public policy issues by virtue of their employment experience. In a 1983 decision, the Court squarely rejected Holmes's reasoning; it stated: "[A] public employee does not relinquish rights to comment on matters of public interest by virtue of government employment."

In a series of cases going back to 1968, the Court has formulated several rules about public employees' free speech rights, which aim to strike an appropriate accommodation between the two competing concerns in this context: on the one hand, the government's (and the public's) interest in efficient government workplaces; and on the other hand, public employees' (and the public's) interest in expression about matters of public concern.

The following is a summary of the First Amendment analysis that applies to a public employee's claim that a government employer has violated the employee's First Amendment rights, with the following caveat: The Court has recognized that the first general rule may not apply to faculty members at public educational institutions, because of the special First Amendment/academic freedom concerns in that context.

1. The threshold question is whether the expression at issue is ordinarily within the scope of the employee's job responsibilities; if so, the employee has no First Amendment rights.

2. If the expression was not within the scope of the employee's job responsibilities, the next question is whether it was about a matter of public concern; if not, the employee has no First Amendment rights.

3. If the expression was about a matter of public concern, the reviewing court undertakes "a delicate balancing of the competing interests surrounding the speech and its consequences." The court will uphold a restriction on this expression only if it concludes that the interest in an efficient workplace outweighs the free expression interests.

To illustrate how these rules play out in specific cases, I will summarize how the Supreme Court enforced each rule in the case in which it announced that rule.

The Court initially articulated the first question—whether the employee speech was within the employee's job duties—in a 2006 case involving an assistant district attorney (ADA) who had been disciplined for writing a memorandum concluding that a police officer had lied in his affidavit supporting a search warrant (which would invalidate the resulting search and criminal conviction to which it led). The Supreme Court held that the ADA had no First Amendment right to engage in this expression because it was pursuant to his job duties.

The Court reasoned: "Restricting speech that owes its existence to a public employee's professional responsibilities does not infringe any liberties the employee might have enjoyed as a private citizen. It simply reflects the exercise of employer control over what the employer itself has commissioned or created." In other words, as the Court amplified in a 2022 decision, "for constitutional purposes," this speech is in effect "the government's own speech."

The above-described 2006 holding built on a central theme throughout the modern Court's cases considering government employees' free speech rights. The Court consistently has distinguished between public employees' speech in their capacity as "citizens"—which they do not forfeit by virtue of becoming public employees—and their speech specifically in their employment capacity, which the government has more latitude to regulate.

The Court initially laid out the second question—whether the employee speech addressed a matter of public concern—in a 1983 case also involving an ADA, who was punished after circulating a questionnaire among other ADAs in the same office, asking about workplace policies. As in other contexts, in assessing whether government employees' speech addresses a matter of public concern, the Court has generally construed that concept broadly. However, in this case, the Court concluded that the expression at issue addressed employee grievances, not public concerns, and hence was not protected by the First Amendment.

Finally, the Court initially set out the third question—whether, on balance, the interests in an efficient government workplace outweigh the countervailing free expression interests—in a 1968 case involving a public school teacher. Since the name of the case was *Pickering v. Board of Education*, this test is often referred to as "*Pickering* balancing." The teacher, Marvin Pickering, had been fired for writing a letter to the editor criticizing the school's fundraising practices. Finding that the letter addressed "issues of public importance" and that it did not interfere with the school's operation, the Court held that the firing violated Pickering's First Amendment rights. The Court has listed the following kinds of demonstrable harm that employee speech would have to cause to warrant its restriction under the *Pickering* test: It "impairs discipline by superiors or harmony among coworkers, has a detrimental impact on close working relationships for which personal loyalty and confidence are necessary, or impedes the performance of the speaker's duties or interferes with the regular operation of the enterprise."

Summarizing the composite rule resulting from this sequence of cases, the Court's above-referenced 2006 decision echoed the general strict scrutiny test, stating that government employers may impose "only those speech restrictions that are necessary . . . to operate efficiently and effectively."

In a 1987 case, the Court stressed that any restriction on public employees' speech about matters of public concern must be viewpoint-neutral, cautioning that "vigilance is necessary to ensure that public employers do not . . . silence [employees'] discourse, not because it hampers public functions but simply because superiors disagree with the content of employees' speech." Accordingly, the Court upheld the free speech rights of a clerical employee in a county constable's office, who made the following statement to a fellow employee after learning that President Ronald Reagan had been shot in an assassination attempt: "If they go for him again, I hope they get him." The Court commented: "The inappropriate or controversial character of a statement is irrelevant to the question whether it deals with a matter of public concern."

What First Amendment rights do prisoners have?

Since prisons' primary concerns include protecting the security and safety of inmates and staff, and since the Court traditionally has deferred to prison officials' expertise about those concerns, it reviews any prison speech restriction under its most deferential standard for reviewing any constitutional rights claim: "rational basis." The Court will uphold any prison speech regulation so long as it is "rationally related" to a legitimate penological interest. (In contrast, speech regulations in the general public sphere are subject to the much more demanding "intermediate" or "strict scrutiny" tests for content-neutral or content-based restrictions, respectively, which require government to demonstrate a tighter connection between the regulation and a weightier government goal.)

Under this lenient standard, the Court consistently has upheld prison speech regulations, even when they stifle important communications to and from inmates—ranging from legal advice, to newspapers and magazines, to family photographs—and even when there is scant if any evidence that they promote prison security interests. In dissenting from a 2006 decision, which completely denied certain inmates access to any secular, nonlegal periodicals, Justice Ruth Bader Ginsburg commented that prison officials had prevailed simply by asserting that "in our professional judgment the restriction is warranted." Consistent with this extremely deferential approach, the Court also has upheld restrictions on journalists who seek access to prisons and prisoners for purposes of informing the public about prison conditions. In consequence, even beyond prisoners themselves, those whose First Amendment rights are foreshortened by these rulings include the specific members of the general public who seek to communicate with prisoners, as well as all members of the general public who seek information about our nation's prisons.

To illustrate the Court's strong deference to prison officials, and the resulting adverse impact on First Amendment rights, I will summarize a 1989 decision, which is typical. In that case, the Court permitted prison authorities to bar inmates from receiving various publications, including *Labyrinth*, a magazine published by the Committee for Prisoner Humanity & Justice. One of the articles it contained, "Medical Murder," described how three Black prisoners at the U.S. Penitentiary in Terre

Haute, Indiana had died of asthma in 1975. The article recounted that the prison infirmary had only one respirator, which had already been broken as of January 1975, and remained broken in August, when the third Black prisoner died of asthma. The Court deferred to prison officials' decision to block the magazine on the ground that this article "would be detrimental to the good order and discipline of this institution," since its "philosophy could . . . cause . . . problems with the Medical Staff."

What First Amendment rights do military personnel have?

Deferential as the Supreme Court has been to prison officials, it has been even more deferential to military authorities when they restrict military personnel's exercise of what would be constitutional rights for civilians. The Court has essentially rubber-stamped any such restriction, accepting without examination military officials' conclusory assertions that the restriction promotes "order and discipline." In terms of constitutional rights, the Court has relegated service members to a status that is both separate and unequal, stating that "the military is, by necessity, a specialized society separate from civilian society."

Consistent with its virtually automatic approval of military restrictions on constitutional rights in general, the Court has invariably upheld military speech restrictions in particular. Its first case on point was *Parker v. Levy*, decided in 1974. Along with so many major free speech cases, this one also centered on expression advocating racial justice. Dr. Howard Levy, an Army captain, urged Black enlisted men to refuse to serve in Vietnam because "they are discriminated against and denied their freedom in the United States, and . . . discriminated against in Vietnam by being given all the hazardous duty and . . . suffering the majority of casualties." Levy was convicted under the Uniform Code of Military Justice (UCMJ) for "conduct unbecoming an officer and a gentleman" and for "disloyal statements" prejudicial to "good order and discipline." If Levy had been a civilian, his speech would have been entitled to special protection, since it addressed matters of public concern. Even if his speech could be construed as advocating illegal conduct (e.g., disobeying military orders), such advocacy is protected for civilians. As the Court unanimously held in the landmark 1969 *Brandenburg* case, even advocacy of illegal conduct is protected; only intentional incitement of imminent illegal conduct, which is likely to happen imminently, is unprotected. Moreover, any civilian law with the sweeping, elastic language in the applicable UCMJ provisions would be struck down as unduly vague and substantially overbroad. Yet, invoking the "specialized society" rationale, the Court rejected Levy's First Amendment claims.

Pursuant to the "specialized society" approach, the Court even has upheld prior restraints against military personnel's expression based on speculative fears that the expression "could affect adversely" "morale, discipline, and . . . order." In civilian society, prior restraints constitute an especially serious First Amendment violation, which are almost automatically unconstitutional. Yet in the military context, the Court even has upheld the type of prior restraint that historically has been the most suspect: a prior licensing requirement. Furthermore, the Court upheld this requirement when it was imposed on military personnel who sought to petition Members of Congress and the Secretary of Defense, an especially important exercise of not only the general First Amendment freedom of speech, but also the specific First Amendment right "to petition the government for a redress of grievances." The Air Force regulations at issue required service members to get their commanders' approval before circulating petitions on Air Force bases. In yet another example of the essential role that free speech plays in racial justice advocacy, the petition challenged grooming regulations that, it maintained, "have caused more racial tension, decrease in morale and retention, and loss of respect for authorities than any other official Air Force policy." Nonetheless, the Supreme Court upheld the prior restraint against this petition.

7

OTHER LEGAL PROTECTIONS FOR FREE SPEECH, IN ADDITION TO THE FIRST AMENDMENT

Beyond the First Amendment, what other sources of U.S. law provide additional protection to free speech?

This book focuses on the First Amendment law that the Supreme Court has generated, because it provides the minimal baseline level of free speech protection, all across the United States, against all officials. It is important to bear in mind, though, that other sources of law provide certain additional speech protections: state constitutional law; legislation by federal, state, or local bodies; and contractual provisions. Consistent with the U.S. Constitution's federalist structure, each of the 50 U.S. states has its own state constitution, which is authoritatively interpreted by its own state high court. Some state high courts have held that their state constitutional counterparts to the First Amendment grant certain additional protection to free speech, beyond what First Amendment law provides. Likewise, lawmaking bodies at all levels may also expand speech protections. Furthermore, individuals and groups of individuals may enter into contracts that provide added speech protection in particular circumstances, and which are legally enforceable under contract law principles.

Under the U.S. Constitution's "Supremacy Clause," the U.S. Constitution is "the supreme law of the land," so any state constitutional ruling, as well as any state statute, that violates the U.S. Constitution would be null and void. This became an issue concerning an important state-high-court ruling extending free speech rights beyond those the U.S. Supreme Court had upheld under the First Amendment. In 1979, the California Supreme Court held that its state constitution required privately owned shopping centers to permit members of the public to engage in expressive conduct on their premises (as private entities, these shopping centers had no First Amendment obligation to do this). The shopping center owners challenged the California Supreme Court's holding as violating their own First Amendment rights— specifically, their freedom not to be compelled to convey the messages of the members of the public—as well as their property rights under the U.S. Constitution. In ruling on that case, the U.S. Supreme Court reaffirmed the state's "sovereign right to adopt in its own Constitution individual liberties more expansive than those conferred by the Federal Constitution," and concluded that the California Supreme Court's holding did not violate either asserted federal constitutional right. If the Justices had reached the opposite conclusion on this key federal law issue— whether the state constitutional provisions, as interpreted by the California Supreme Court, violated a federal constitutional right—they would have overturned the state high court's ruling.

Below I cite further examples of increased free speech protection that the other sources of law outlined above have provided, beyond contemporary First Amendment law.

What protections do state constitutions and state supreme court decisions provide?

The Free Speech Clause (along with almost all rights-protecting provisions in the U.S. Constitution) extends only to government officials/bodies, not to private sector actors, with only narrow exceptions. In contrast, some state high courts have interpreted their state constitutional counterparts of the Free Speech Clause as extending to at least some private sector entities and actions, as illustrated by the California Supreme Court holding that the preceding answer referenced. The New Jersey Supreme Court likewise has held that the free speech guarantee in New Jersey's constitution extends to private sector entities, including private universities and privately owned shopping centers. As a result of these rulings, members of the general public have the same viewpoint-neutral rights to leaflet, picket, and engage in other expressive conduct in certain areas of these private institutions as they would have in a "traditional public forum"—namely, the open areas that are analogous to public sidewalks, streets, and parks.

What protections do statutes provide?

Federal, state, and local statutes may secure essentially any protections for free speech that are deemed desirable—subject to general constitutional constraints upon their lawmaking power. Given the many recent campus free speech controversies, one noteworthy example is California's 1992 "Leonard Law," which secures at private secular educational institutions the same free speech rights that the First Amendment guarantees at public educational institutions. In 1995, a California judge held that this law was violated by the hate speech restrictions that Stanford University had adopted. In light of many recent situations in which private sector employees have been fired for controversial social media posts or other communications, also noteworthy are the various federal and state statutes that provide some protection for employees' free speech.

What protections do contracts provide?

A contract is a binding agreement, which can be enforced in court. The principles of contract law require enforceable contracts to comply with certain broad substantive legal requirements (e.g., the parties must have a "meeting of the minds" and mutually rely on each others' undertakings) but the law is flexible in terms of format details. For example, most contracts don't even need to be in writing at all, let alone contain formal written elements, such as the parties' signatures.

Any individual or group of individuals can enter into contracts with anyone else for the purpose of protecting free speech rights. For instance, in negotiating a collective bargaining agreement for the employees it represents, a labor union could insist that the employer respect certain free speech rights for the employees. Likewise, star athletes or entertainers could negotiate individual employment contracts that secured their free speech rights.

Another important example of contractually protected free speech rights involves private higher education institutions. Most of them voluntarily choose to protect the same free speech and academic freedom rights on the part of their students and faculty members that the First Amendment requires public universities to enforce. Consistent with their educational and research missions, these private universities typically set out their free speech/academic freedom commitments in generally available documents such as faculty handbooks, student handbooks, and websites. For example, in 2014 the University of Chicago—a private institution—adopted a set of speech-protective principles that are now generally referred to as "the Chicago Principles," and which have been adopted by many other private universities and colleges. Courts have often held that these kinds of publicly announced pledges of support for free speech give rise to enforceable contracts, binding the university vis-à-vis students and faculty members. The key rationale is that, in choosing to join a particular campus community, these individuals have relied upon those free speech pledges, as the campus officials intended them to do.

8

SOME IMPORTANT CURRENT FREE SPEECH ISSUES

What is "cancel culture"?

Legal protections for freedom of speech are necessary, but not sufficient, to create conditions in which free speech can maximally flourish: where all members of our society enjoy actual and equal opportunities to express themselves, and to participate in discussions about public issues, no matter who they are, and no matter what they believe. Public opinion surveys indicate that many people do not exercise their legal free speech rights because they fear adverse reactions by their peers or other members of our society, including online mobs. These reactions include calling for and imposing various punitive sanctions on the speaker, such as social ostracism and even the loss of jobs or expulsion from school.

Far from violating speakers' First Amendment free speech rights, even the harshest criticism of speakers and their ideas, including advocacy that they be harshly punished, constitutes the critics' exercise of *their* free speech rights. Yet the term "cancel culture" captures the concern that some criticism is disproportionately harsh, and has an unduly speech-suppressive impact on not only the directly targeted speaker, but also countless others. Surveys indicate that substantial percentages of all of us, across the political and demographic spectrums, are deterred from voicing certain views, or even from addressing whole subjects, for fear that we might face such harsh consequences. These surveys do not focus on speech that most of us believe should be self-censored, such as targeted racist or other epithets directed at another person. Rather, they concern general expressions of opinion, or even asking questions, about complex public policy issues, including those involving racial justice, gender equality, abortion, police reform, immigration, and pandemic measures.

Nourishing a culture that encourages both robust free speech and robust counterspeech, while avoiding unduly harsh and intimidating advocacy on either side, entails the proverbial "delicate balance." After all, robust free speech itself may have the same intimidating, chilling impact that harsh counterspeech does. That is an important concern that prompts calls for non-emergency restrictions on hate speech, for example. Advocates of such restrictions correctly observe that hate speech may well have a silencing impact on not only those directly targeted, but also others within the disparaged group. For this reason, opponents of non-emergency hate speech restrictions—including the author of this book—expressly advocate vigorous, proactive counterspeech to deter hate speech. But here's the tough question: "When does counterspeech go too far?" A thoughtful, nuanced answer was provided by Suzanne Nossel, CEO of the free speech organization PEN America:

> You can firmly reject a speaker's message without demanding that he or she suffer for it. Even if the [speaker] deserves no sympathy, when social ostracization becomes demonization and dehumanization, it debases our discourse writ large . . .
>
> Digital discourse affords us the collective power to justifiably inhibit speakers from voicing noxious views. But it also allows us to silence countless others who may

withhold original ideas or provocative perspectives because they fear toxic, virulent blowback. . . .
    Ultimately, the purpose of counterspeech should
not be to exact retribution or to humiliate, but rather to
persuade.

Just as counterspeech—not government censorship—is the
appropriate response to hate speech (and other controversial speech), counterspeech—not government censorship—
is also the appropriate response to unduly harsh anti-hate
counterspeech. Counterspeech is an imperfect tool: In some
instances, as Nossel expounds, it suppresses non-targeted,
non-harmful speech; additionally, in other instances, it does
not sufficiently suppress the harmful speech that it does target.
Nonetheless, counterspeech holds both more promise and less
peril than government censorship.

What are the free speech rights of social media companies and their users?

Many politicians, lawyers, tech experts, and others have been
actively examining and debating the complicated question of
what free speech rights *should be* for social media companies
and their users, and they have proposed various new laws on
point, some of which have been enacted. In contrast, until recently there has been a broad consensus among experts about
what these free speech rights currently *are* under existing First
Amendment doctrine. Recently, though, there has been some
disagreement on this matter too.
    Consistent with the "state action doctrine," social media
companies, as private sector entities, have no general First
Amendment obligation to honor free speech rights of anyone who uses their platforms, or seeks to do so. Moreover,
along with traditional media, social media have their own
First Amendment rights to decide which speech and speakers

they will host on their platforms, and which they will not. Accordingly, the social media companies may adopt whatever "content moderation" policies or "community standards" they choose.

Notwithstanding the fact that users (and would-be users) of giant tech platforms have no First Amendment right to voice their views on such platforms, as a practical matter, meaningful free speech requires access to such platforms. In a 2017 decision, the U.S. Supreme Court declared: "While in the past there may have been difficulty in identifying the most important places . . . for the exchange of views, today the answer is clear. It is cyberspace . . . and social media in particular." Among other things, the Court recognized, social media are the most essential platforms for debate and discussion about public affairs and public officials among "We the People," and for us to engage with officials and candidates. This makes it vital for our democracy to maintain the same "uninhibited, robust, and wide-open" free speech in these new venues that the Court has historically shielded in traditional venues.

In sum, we now face the worst of both worlds when it comes to online companies' censorial power over everyone else's speech. As the Supreme Court acknowledged, these companies wield power over speech of a magnitude that in the past has only been exercised by governments. Yet they exercise this power unconstrained by the First Amendment and other constitutional checks that limit government power, but not private sector power.

Some people whose messages have been removed from social media platforms, or otherwise treated unfavorably (e.g., by having warning labels attached), or who have been barred from platforms altogether, have invoked the "entanglement" exception to the state action doctrine. When an action by a private sector actor involves a sufficiently close "entanglement" or relationship with the government, then the ostensibly private action is treated as tantamount to government action and subject to the same First Amendment constraints that bind the government itself. In each situation in which the entanglement exception is alleged, the court must make a fact-specific determination whether the purportedly private action in fact resulted from enough government pressure or collaboration. At the time I am writing this answer (May 2023), no court has yet ruled that any challenged social media content moderation decision did come within the entanglement exception. Some courts have rejected that contention on the factual record in the specific cases they adjudicated, and others have ruled that the plaintiffs have alleged adequate factual grounds for this claim to be entitled to engage in the "discovery" process—seeking pertinent information from the companies and the government in an effort to substantiate their claims.

Recently two states—Florida and Texas—have enacted statutes that impose certain restrictions on tech companies' content moderation policies, thus squarely challenging the hitherto prevailing assumption that such restrictions violate the companies' First Amendment rights. The tech companies immediately filed lawsuits seeking to bar the statutes' implementation on First Amendment grounds. The two federal appellate courts that ruled on these cases reached opposite results; the companies' First Amendment argument was accepted in the Florida case, but rejected in the Texas case (over a dissenting opinion). The Supreme Court has not yet made any substantive rulings on these questions. Several Justices have issued individual opinions indicating their inclinations—although not necessarily conclusions—on point. The most extensive such discussion to date was in a 2021 opinion by Justice Thomas (not joined by any other Justice), suggesting that the Court should consider permitting government regulation of tech platforms' content moderation on one or more of several theories, which would override the companies' First Amendment claims: that the companies could be considered common carriers, public utilities, and/or public accommodations, and hence required to serve as neutral conduits for third parties' communications. In 2022, Justice Alito wrote an opinion, joined by Justices Thomas and Gorsuch, indicating their openness to reexamining First Amendment principles and precedents in the social media context.

The Supreme Court has almost complete discretion about whether to review particular cases, so it is unpredictable when the Court might choose to address these thorny issues. On the one hand, given the disagreement between the two federal appellate courts that recently have ruled on these important issues, the Supreme Court might choose to address them soon. On the other hand, concerning issues of such complexity, the Court sometimes prefers to await further rulings and analysis by additional federal appellate courts before weighing in itself.

What is Section 230?

In addition to the social media companies' First Amendment rights, their free speech rights have been reinforced by a federal statute that was enacted in 1996, shortly after the internet had garnered widespread political and public attention. Commonly referred to as "Section 230," this short section of a comprehensive communications law contains two provisions. The first states: "No provider or user of an interactive computer service shall be treated as the publisher or speaker of any information provided by another information content provider." With a few exceptions, this provision generally shields any online entity that hosts third-party content, including social media companies, from liability for the third-party content. Without this liability shield, online intermediaries would be forced to serve as strict gatekeepers, analogous to newspaper editors or TV producers, allowing only hand-picked, carefully curated third-party content, or perhaps no third-party content at all. Such an approach would have thwarted the internet's unique potential as "the most participatory form of mass speech yet developed," to quote one of the first court opinions about online free speech rights. For this reason, this first provision in Section 230 has been celebrated as "the 26 words that created the Internet." Section 230's second provision states that online services are not liable for "any action voluntarily taken in good faith to restrict access to or availability of material that the provider or user considers to be obscene, lewd, lascivious, filthy, excessively violent, harassing, or otherwise objectionable, whether or not such material is constitutionally protected." Just as the first provision shields online intermediaries from liability for any decision to host third-party content, the second provision shields them from liability for any decision *not* to host third-party content. The purpose was to permit companies to implement content moderation policies that would encourage user participation, recognizing that users might prefer not to encounter the full panoply of speech that the First Amendment protects. Content moderation policies could include, for instance, blocking spam and blocking certain violent images.

Although political, media, and public discussion of Section 230 focuses on its immunity shield for tech giants, it is important to note that Section 230 also applies to any online site that includes third-party content, such as individual blogs and websites that have comment sections. The Electronic Frontier Foundation, which defends civil liberties in the digital world, explains that Section 230 "has allowed . . . YouTube and Vimeo users to upload their own videos, Amazon and Yelp to offer countless user reviews, [and] craigslist to host classified ads."

Section 230 was passed by overwhelming majorities of both Houses of Congress, supported by Democrats and Republicans alike. In recent years, however, many officials of both parties have complained about social media companies' content moderation policies, and have proposed legislation that would substantially revise Section 230, or even repeal it altogether. That said, officials' criticisms of content moderation policies are very diverse, and even inconsistent with each other. Many Republicans complain that the companies discriminate against conservative speech and speakers, whereas many Democrats complain that the companies do not sufficiently block conservative speech that the complainants view as hate speech, disinformation/misinformation, or extremist/terrorist speech.

In contrast with many politicians of both major parties, many free speech and human rights advocates oppose revising or repealing Section 230. They maintain that such a move would thwart free speech for the unprecedented millions of people who have been availing themselves of the unparalleled opportunity to exchange information and ideas online, including human rights activists and political dissidents.

What are some current major threats to free speech?

From a worldwide perspective, the threats to free speech include the most direct and total suppression: the execution and assassination of journalists and others who dare to question prevailing political and religious orthodoxies in authoritarian and theocratic regimes. The Committee to Protect Journalists (CPJ) reported that in 2022, at least 41 journalists and media workers worldwide were killed in retaliation for their work (CPJ is investigating 26 other such killings in 2022 to determine whether they were work-related), while an additional 363 reporters were imprisoned for their work.

Although these blatant, brutal attacks on speakers/speech might seem remote from the United States, a recent tragedy reveals that, to the contrary, they reach directly into the heart of our country. I am writing these words only two weeks after author Salman Rushdie was repeatedly stabbed and severely injured as he was preparing to speak at the Chautauqua Institution in western New York State—a bucolic rural community, which is specifically dedicated to open inquiry and discourse. This assault, with its profound life-impairing consequences—including Rushdie's loss of sight in one eye and the use of one hand—was apparently in retribution for his staunch defense of the freedom to write on behalf of dissident writers in many countries, as well as his own writings that some Islamic leaders have condemned. Ironically, Rushdie was attacked just as he was about to present remarks extolling the United States' special role in affording a refuge to writers who have been persecuted elsewhere. Yes, Rushdie and other writers have fortunately enjoyed more freedom and safety in the United States than in other parts of the world, but alas: far from enough.

The long hands of the world's most repressive, censorial regimes have had additional stifling impacts on free speech right here in the United States. One horrific example is the 2018 assassination and dismemberment of the dissident Saudi journalist Jamal Khashoggi, who was a columnist for the *Washington Post*, by Saudi government agents, allegedly at the behest of Crown Prince Mohammed bin Salman. Free speech in the U.S. also has been suppressed by the threatened and actual violence in many countries by certain Muslims who objected to works including Rushdie's *The Satanic Verses*, the Danish newspaper *Jyllands-Posten's* "Danish cartoons," and the French satirical magazine *Charlie Hebdo's* cartoons. In light of these incidents, U.S. publishers and booksellers have declined to distribute these works for fear of violent reprisals here at home, as well as in other countries. I will cite just some examples of this widespread self-censorship, which has deprived U.S. residents of vital art, information, and ideas:

- U.S. publishers declined to publish the paperback edition of *The Satanic Verses*.
- Yale University Press, which published a book about the Danish cartoon controversy in 2009, declined to include the cartoons in the book.
- When covering the mass murders of *Charlie Hebdo* cartoonists in 2015, leading U.S. newspapers, including the *New York Times*, declined to reprint the cartoons for which these cartoonists had died.
- In 2012, when a YouTube video that was critical of Islam was blamed (wrongly, as it turned out) for having

instigated the deadly attack on the U.S. embassy in Benghazi, Libya, prominent U.S. officials pressured YouTube to censor the video.

Beyond such extraterritorial censorial inroads into the United States, which originate in some of the world's most autocratic regimes and intolerant groups, we have no shortage of the homegrown variety, coming from all possible sources: from government officials all across the political spectrum, and also private sector forces, ranging from powerful tech titans to Twittermobs, and also reflecting ideologically diverse views. In this response to this book's last question, I will now revisit an answer to one of its first questions, which explained why "freedom of speech for thee" is inextricable from "freedom of speech for me." The rationales that are offered for non-emergency speech restrictions on particular speakers or ideas inevitably are recycled in different factual contexts, including when political power changes hands, in an effort to legitimate such restrictions on diametrically different speakers and ideas. In the United States, many conservatives and Republicans have mocked campus calls to shield left-leaning students from ideas that they find "divisive" or that make them "uncomfortable," deriding the students as "snowflakes." Yet many of the same conservatives and Republicans have appropriated those very concepts in actual and proposed state laws all over the country, which bar the inclusion of ideas that K–12 students (and sometimes also college/university students) find "divisive," or that make them "uncomfortable."

I could recite numerous additional specific free speech threats, ranging from burgeoning state laws that seek to curb rights of peaceful protesters (which tend to be supported mostly by conservatives and Republicans); to successful campaigns to halt the publication or distribution of works that are deemed to constitute "cultural appropriation," or to perpetuate the "White Savior myth," or to challenge certain predominant progressive views on social and cultural issues (which tend to be supported mostly by progressives and Democrats); to calls to eliminate First Amendment and statutory limitations on tech platforms' liability for third-party content, thus denying most people the presumptively unfettered access—subject to content moderation policies—to convey and receive ideas that such immunity has fostered (which tend to be supported by officials and citizens across the political spectrum).

Although the specific threats will continue to change, experience demonstrates that one overridingly important pattern will persist: These threats will continue to emanate from all points on the political spectrum. For that reason, I want to conclude this answer—and this book—by describing the single greatest general threat to free speech—past, present, and future: ignorance about freedom of speech, including the core viewpoint-neutrality principle, and ignorance about the incalculable benefits that this freedom has bestowed upon individuals and society alike. If you are unaware of the essential role that this precious right has played in your life, you may not even realize when it has been violated, and you will not demand that it be respected, with the result that the right will atrophy, not only for you, but also for others.

CONCLUSION

No matter what your previous understandings of and perspectives about freedom of speech might have been before you consulted this book, I hope they have been expanded by your grappling with the book's questions and answers. I deliberately use the phrase "grappling with," rather than the more passive term "reading," because my aim has been to stimulate your active critical thinking, making you more than passive recipients of the book's contents, but rather inspiring you to undertake and continue your own engagement with these perennially important, challenging issues. I hope that this book has served the same function as the appetizer course in a meal: providing some nourishment, but still leaving you hungry for more "food for thought."

I also hope that the information this book has laid out, as well as the thought processes it has propelled, will encourage all readers to more actively exercise your own hard-won freedom of speech, including by advocating for your own understandings of what that freedom means concerning specific public controversies. Whatever your views might be about free speech—or anything else—you should exercise your own free speech rights to advocate for those views: Speak, write, organize, demonstrate, and petition! In short, I hope all readers will vigorously exercise our most precious right of all: the right *not* to remain silent.

NOTES

Acknowledgments

  1 Additional material, which has not been included in this book for the sake of brevity, can be found at https://www.nyls.edu/faculty/nadine-strossen/. This material includes citations for quoted language and a list of further readings.

Chapter 1

  1 Even more longstanding are Virginia's 1776 Declaration of Rights, which protects press freedom, and the 1789 French Declaration of the Rights of Man and the Citizen, which forms part of the French constitution and protects freedom of opinion and expression.

  2 Although the First Amendment also protects other rights, the phrase "First Amendment" tends to be used in everyday parlance to refer specifically to its free expression guarantee; this book does likewise.

Chapter 2

  1 The Supreme Court has said that speech regulations based on a speaker's "specific motivating ideology or . . . opinion or perspective"—that is, viewpoint-based regulations—constitute an especially "egregious form of content discrimination," but all content-based regulations are subject to the same strict First Amendment standards. Therefore, this book generally refers to viewpoint- and content-based restrictions interchangeably.

  2 The *fatwa*, as a solicitation to commit specific crimes against specific individuals, satisfies the emergency principle—by

directly facilitating imminent serious harm—and hence does not constitute protected speech under the First Amendment.

3 This is an abbreviation of the term "Netzwerkdurchsetzungsgesetz," which is commonly translated as the "Network Enforcement Act."

4 Even incarceration won't necessarily suppress hatemongers' expression, however; their websites can well remain active. For example, Ernst Zundel, a purveyor of neo-Nazi propaganda, was prosecuted, convicted, and imprisoned for engaging in hate speech in both Canada and Germany as a result of protracted litigation, from 1996 to 2007. As one expert pointed out in 2010, though, "Even now, Zundel's website is still running and regularly updated with his 'letters from prison' despite his incarceration."

Chapter 3

1 The Court long has held that the "speech" that the First Amendment shields includes certain nonverbal communicative or symbolic conduct, such as marching in a parade or wearing an armband. I use the term "expressive conduct" to encompass both verbal and nonverbal conduct that is communicative; after all, even the most quintessential forms of speech—talking and writing—involve conduct.

2 In a 1925 decision, the Supreme Court declared that the First Amendment's free speech guarantee, which directly binds only federal officials, is also indirectly binding on state and local governments. That decision embraced the "incorporation doctrine," which reads the broad language of the Fourteenth Amendment's Due Process Clause (providing that states may not "deprive any person of life, liberty, or property, without due process of law") as "incorporating" certain fundamental rights, making them enforceable against state/local officials.

3 In contrast, in its pre-modern era, the Court for 37 years held that motion pictures were entitled to no First Amendment protection at all. In its first decision about the then-new film medium, in 1915 the Court held that "the exhibition of moving pictures is a business, not to be regarded . . . as part of the press." Therefore, the Court permitted state and local governments to operate film censorship boards, and many did so, even subjecting films to the most onerous form of censorship: prior restraint through

licensing requirements. Not until 1952 did the Court overturn this 1915 decision and enforce First Amendment protections for films. The Court's 1952 decision unanimously struck down New York's ban on a film deemed "sacrilegious" (the 1948 Italian film "The Miracle," by the acclaimed director Roberto Rossellini, about a devout peasant girl who believes that she is the Virgin Mary, whose pregnancy resulted from "immaculate conception," leading the contemptuous townsfolk to drive her out of town).

4 The sole exception is Justice John Paul Stevens.

5 "Congress shall make no law respecting an establishment of religion, or prohibiting the free exercise thereof."

6 Some Justices reject the concept of "substantive due process," whereby the Due Process Clauses of the Fifth and Fourteenth Amendments have been construed to protect certain implicit rights concerning sexual and family matters, including the right to use contraception and formerly the right to choose an abortion. Critics of substantive due process stress that the Due Process Clauses' language explicitly refers solely to procedural rights; they provide that government may not "deprive" anyone "of life, liberty, or property, without due process of law." In contrast, these same Justices construe the First Amendment to encompass unenumerated rights that complement and support the substantive rights that it explicitly lays out.

7 The author of this book directly benefited from the holding regarding the Jaycees. After the Supreme Court required that organization to admit women, in 1986 it changed its longstanding "Ten Outstanding Young Men" award to the "Ten Outstanding Young Americans" award, and I was one of the first three women to receive this new award in 1986.

8 In other words, if the services were sought by a heterosexual friend of a gay couple, who was assisting in planning their same-sex wedding, the services would be denied; conversely, if the services were sought by a gay friend of a heterosexual couple, who was assisting in planning their wedding, the services would be provided.

9 As this book is being completed (in May 2023), two cases are pending before the Supreme Court, which it will likely decide in June 2023, and which many experts believe will strike down race-based affirmative action programs for higher education admissions, regardless of this academic freedom rationale.

10 This is an acronym for the "Development, Relief, and Education for Alien Minors Act," a proposed federal law, which would extend some legal protections to certain unauthorized immigrants who entered the United States as minors.

Chapter 4

1 The U.S. legal system has permitted some speech that causes similar emotional or psychic harms to be punished through civil tort actions for "intentional infliction of emotional distress." As a later answer discusses, tort law defines this concept very narrowly, and the Supreme Court has imposed additional First Amendment limits on it.

2 In some pre-modern cases, the Court used the phrase "clear and present danger" to summarize the standard for restricting speech based on its harmful potential. Construed literally, this phrase could be understood to embody the emergency principle. However, the pre-modern Court repeatedly invoked a much-diluted (mis)interpretation of the phrase to uphold speech restrictions based on speculative dangers that were neither "clear" nor "present." Therefore, the modern Court has abandoned this pre-modern terminology.

3 The outlawed material is sometimes described by the misleading term "harmful to minors," thus inaccurately connoting a broader concept of expressive material, beyond obscenity as to minors, with its exclusively sexual focus. To the contrary, the Court has broadly upheld minors' free speech rights concerning speech with all other (i.e., non-sexual) content.

4 The Court acknowledged the possibility that "some categories of speech that have been historically unprotected . . . have not yet been specifically identified or discussed . . . in our case law." However, the Court stressed that the government would have to show "persuasive evidence that a novel restriction on content is part of a long (if heretofore unrecognized) tradition of proscription." Since this 2010 decision, the Court has consistently concluded that the government has failed to make such a showing, rejecting multiple government efforts to do so regarding various types of controversial speech, including violent video games marketed to minors, speech that supports terrorism, depictions of animal cruelty, and false claims of having received military honors.

5   The First Amendment protects other expressive material that
    also records abusive, illegal conduct, including videotaped
    images of police brutality and terrorist attacks. In distinguishing
    child pornography from this other material, the Court not only
    stressed the exceptional importance of protecting children, but
    also concluded that child pornography "presented a special
    case" because "[t]he market for [it] was intrinsically related
    to the underlying abuse, and was therefore an integral part
    of the production of such materials." The Court accepted the
    government's argument that, given the "low profile, clandestine"
    nature of the child pornography production process, it was
    difficult to prosecute those engaged in it, and therefore "the most
    expeditious, if not the only practical" way to prevent the child
    abuse that the pornography depicts is to "dry up the market"
    for it.
6   The Virginia Supreme Court also concluded that this state statute
    was not undermined by the U.S. Supreme Court's 1973 *Roe*
    decision, because *Roe* did not "mention . . . abortion advertising."
7   The Court also has occasionally used the term "designated
    public forum" to denote public property other than traditional
    public forums, which the government has chosen to designate
    as being available for some free speech uses. Such designated
    forums are functionally identical to limited public forums, since
    the government is unlikely to make any property (other than
    traditional public forums) available for all speakers on all topics.
    In other words, when the government designates property as a
    forum, it will almost certainly set it up as a limited public forum.
8   A speech regulation that satisfies the emergency principle
    logically also satisfies the viewpoint-neutrality requirement. An
    emergency regulation by definition targets speech because it
    directly, imminently causes or threatens specific serious harm.
    It therefore does not target speech solely due to disfavor of its
    content. In short, these core principles are the proverbial "two
    sides of the same coin."
9   Additionally, some RTLM broadcasts may have constituted
    punishable incitement. In contrast, RTLM also broadcast some
    hateful anti-Tutsi propaganda that would not be punishable
    under the emergency principle.

10   Mitchell was convicted of assault under a "hate crime" or "bias
     crime" statute, and the Supreme Court rejected Mitchell's First
     Amendment challenge to that statute.
11   Mr. Lewis testified that Officer Berner's first words were: " 'Let
     me see your god damned license. I'll show you that you can't
     follow the police all over the streets.' " Mr. Lewis's testimony
     continued: "[Mrs. Lewis] got out [of the truck] and said 'Officer,
     I want to find out about my son.' He said 'you get in the car,
     woman. Get your black ass in the god damned car or I will show
     you something.' " Mrs. Lewis testified that she had not used "any
     profanity toward the officer."
12   Some laws single out "discriminatory harassment" for enhanced
     punishment, consistent with the general concept of "hate crimes"
     or "bias crimes."
13   Certain expression in employment and educational settings may
     also be punished as yet another type of harassment, "quid pro
     quo harassment." This is a type of extortion (which is a context-
     based category of speech that satisfies the emergency principle);
     for example, a professor tells a student that he will give her a
     better grade if she sleeps with him.

Chapter 5
 1   In contrast, the Court has held that the First Amendment
     excludes a subset of sexual expression, known by the legal term
     of art "obscenity," which is defined solely in terms of its content.
     This controversial "obscenity exception" is now the only content-
     based category of speech excluded from First Amendment
     protection.
 2   "Misinformation"designates speech that is intentionally false.
 3   In *Sullivan* itself, for example, none of the insignificant factual
     inaccuracies that gave rise to the enormous, speech-chilling
     damages altered the general thrust of the advertisement at
     issue, protesting Southern officials' unlawful obstruction of
     pro–civil rights activism. The punished inaccuracies include
     the following: "Negro students" who participated in a
     demonstration at the South Carolina State Capitol "sang the
     National Anthem and not 'My Country, 'Tis of Thee' "; "although
     nine students were expelled . . . , this was not for leading
     the demonstration . . . , but for demanding service at a lunch

counter"; and "Dr. King had not been arrested seven times, but only four."

4   To be sure, even the most heavy-handed censorship efforts have not succeeded in completely suppressing targeted words, let alone targeted ideas, thanks to the universal, eternal human aspiration toward free expression, and the associated elasticity of our language. This is a reason why censorship will likely fail to materially promote its goals. Nonetheless, any censorial effort does suppress some speech, with the accompanying stultifying effect upon some ideas, for some people—including not only those whose speech is directly punished, but also the innumerable others whose speech is chilled.

5   Christakis's wife Erika, also a Yale professor who shared the faculty-in-residence duties, had been subject to intemperate student tirades as well. Notably, both Christakises defended the free speech rights of all of their student critics.

6   According to the influential Restatement (Second) of Torts, for any conduct—including expressive conduct—to constitute IIED, the conduct must be "so outrageous in character, and so extreme in degree, as to go beyond all possible bounds of decency, and to be regarded as atrocious, and utterly intolerable in a civilized community"; additionally, "the distress [it caused] must be so severe that no reasonable [person] could be expected to endure it."

7   The 2023 equivalent is about $4.8 million.

8   The Court coined the legal term of art "actual malice" to summarize this requirement. That term is doubly misleading, however: it does not connote the "knowing or reckless" standard, and it implies that the plaintiff must show that the defendant acted with a "malicious" or evil intent, which is not the case.

INDEX

For the benefit of digital users, indexed terms that span two pages (e.g., 52–53) may, on occasion, appear on only one of those pages
Page numbers followed by n. indicate endnotes.

blasphemy, 197–99
Bluman v. FEC (2012), 107–9
B. L. v. Mahanoy (2021), 213–14
book banning, 176–77, 179–80. *See
    also* library books
Borovoy, Alan, 56
Boy Scouts of America (BSA),
    99–100
Brandeis, Louis, 28, 113–14
Brandenburg v. Ohio (1969), 160,
    223–24
Brennan, William, 94, 153–54
Bro, Susan, 31
broadcast restrictions, 143–45
Brown v. Board of Education (1954,
    1955), 84
Buckley v. Valeo (1976), 84–85
Burger, Warren, 192–93, 209–10
Butler v. The Queen (1992), 179–80

Calhoun, John C., 201–2
California state constitution, 226
Calleros, Charles, 58
campaign finance, 84–87, 107–8,
    125–26
campus hate speech codes, 58
Canada, 179–80
Canadian Civil Liberties
    Association, 56
cancel culture, 229–31
Cantwell, Jesse, 192
Cantwell v. Connecticut (1940), 192
capital crimes, 48
Carpenter, Dale, 14
censorship. *See also* First
    Amendment, speech
    restrictions permitted by;
    non-emergency speech
    restrictions
    consensus on, 1–2
    content-based regulations as,
    147–48
    effectiveness of counterspeech
    in comparison to, 63–64

failure of, 249n.4
    most dangerous, outlawed by
    First Amendment, 114–15
    promoting constructive debates
    about, 2–3
    self-censorship, 237–38
    unconstitutional, 25
Chafee, Zechariah, 111
Chaplinsky v. New Hampshire
    (1942), 122–24, 132–33, 161
Charlie Hebdo, 237
Chemerinsky, Erwin, 99–100, 117–
    18, 151–52
Chicago Principles, 194, 228
child pornography, 127, 134–35,
    247n.5
children. *See* minors
Christakis, Erika, 249n.5
Christakis, Nicholas, 196, 249n.5
Cicero, Illinois, 53–54
citizens
    free speech rights of non-U.S.,
    107–9
Citizens United v. FEC (2010), 102–
    3, 104, 108–9, 146–47
civil rights, 10, 50–52, 59–60,
    174–75, 181, 183–84, 203–4,
    248n.3. *See also* equality
    rights
Claiborne Hardware v. NAACP
    (1982), 51–52, 160
"clear and present danger," 246n.2
Cohen, Paul, 193–94
Cohen v. California (1971), 120–21,
    192–94
Cole, David, 181
colleges and universities.
    See also government
    institutions, First Amendment
    rights in special-purpose
    campus hate speech codes, 58
    free speech zones at, 150
    hate speech codes enacted at,
    156–57